Praise for

Why I Find You Irritating

"*Why I Find You Irritating* is an insightful look at generational misperceptions and how our messages can get lost in translation at work. Chris dives into understanding how we can ease tensions and have clearer communication in the multigenerational workplace. This book can help anyone at any age see a new perspective!"

Marshall Goldsmith

New York Times bestselling author of *Triggers*, *Mojo*, and *What Got You Here Won't Get You There*

"Generational differences have most certainly existed in the past and in many cultures, but as we live longer and the cycles of technology and its cultural and media impact continue to accelerate, we are now working in environments in which more and more markedly different generational cohorts need to collaborate and empathize with each other. *Why I Find You Irritating* is a well-researched, informed, and fun-to-read book that provides useful tools and frameworks to assist contemporary workforce environments in becoming more effective."

Jorge Cauz

CEO, Encyclopaedia Britannica Group

"Just when you think that there is nothing new to say about navigating generational differences, Chris De Santis delivers a fresh and provocative perspective on how we view, approach, and traverse generational differences and similarities in the workplace. This book is a must read for anybody who wants to leverage the power of generational diversity to create better teams, organizations, and workplace relationships."

Mary Abbajay

Author of *Managing Up: How to Move Up, Win at Work, and Succeed with Any Type of Boss*

"We have more generations in the workplace than ever before, but that shouldn't be a cause of friction. Instead, it's an opportunity. This book will show you how to embrace generational differences and resolve generational conflict when you can . . . or leverage it when you can't."

David Burkus

Author of *Under New Management: How Leading Organizations Are Upending Business as Usual*

"*Why I Find You Irritating* is a thoughtful, smart, funny, and engaging read. With Chris's usual combination of humor and insight, he reminds us about our generational biases. Regardless of our generational identities—and for that matter, our gender, race, ethnic, and other social identities—we all benefit from understanding where others come from and what they need to get their jobs done well. *Why I Find You Irritating* is an important book, providing useful tips and suggestions to overcome generational differences and ways to create workplaces where we can all thrive."

Andie Kramer

Co-author of *Breaking through Bias (2nd Ed): Communication Techniques for Women to Succeed at Work* and *It's Not You, It's the Workplace: Women's Conflict at Work and the Bias that Built It*

"Not only do I love the title *Why I Find You Irritating*, I appreciate Chris's explanations of how our generational misconceptions can negatively color our perceptions of others. His suggestions for bridging differences are both practical and necessary for getting along in a multigenerational workplace."

Michelle Tillis Lederman

Author of *The Connector's Advantage: 7 Mindsets to Grow Your Influence and Impact*

"Chris De Santis always writes with wit and keen insight, and this book about bridging generational differences at work is no exception. Employers would be wise to heed the suggestions he offers about how to improve workplace mentoring."

Ida Abbott

Author of *The Lawyer's Guide to Mentoring and Sponsoring Women: What Men Need to Know*

"Chris's insights on generational differences and inclusion shape how I think about leading transformational change in a workplace with four generations of talent. His book delivers the thoughtful, direct, and actionable guidance we need to adapt and thrive. I am excited so many others are now empowered to build upon his expertise and wisdom."

Jason Barnwell
Assistant General Counsel, Microsoft Corporation

"We all face challenging communication scenarios that can feel out of our control. In *Why I Find You Irritating*, Chris offers a range of relatable stories and actionable advice so you can better navigate generational friction in the workplace that can drive misunderstandings."

Judi Holler
Bestselling author of *Fear Is My Homeboy: How to Slay Doubt, Boss Up, and Succeed on Your Own Terms*

"I have spent the better part of my career working to further the causes of diversity, equity, and inclusion. Chris is a kindred spirit. I have had the pleasure of working with him on this mission. He is part of my faculty at the Leadership Council on Legal Diversity. His explanations of generational differences and how to accept and embrace them are a gateway and model for understanding and accepting the benefits of diversity and inclusion in all its forms. His book on the topic is worth a look, it is concise, insightful, and at times quite entertaining."

Robert Grey
President, Leadership Council on Legal Diversity (LCLD)

"Chris De Santis carefully leads us to explore the many chambers and layers of the ever-changing generational box we inhabit in the workplace and elsewhere in life. Through his entertaining and well-researched writing, he educates and informs, and even challenges the way in which we interpret this book!"

Ted Acosta
Regional Managing Partner for a global professional services firm

"My company uses Chris as a featured speaker at industry conferences and through a video series on our website. Now he is in print. Anyone who wants to understand how to make generational differences an organizational asset instead of a problem needs to read this book."

Abram Claude
Head of Consultative Services, Columbia Threadneedle Investments

"This is not just a book about corporate hierarchy. It's an owner's manual on how to be a successful human being. Chris writes about complicated dynamics with clarity and manages to make it interesting. If you deal have to deal with people, and we all do, then read this book."

John Riggi
Television writer/director

www.amplifypublishing.com

Why I Find You Irritating: Navigating Generational Friction at Work

Third Printing. This Amplify Publishing edition printed in 2023.

For more information, please contact Amplify Publishing Group:
620 Herndon Parkway #320
Herndon, VA 20170
info@amplifypublishing.com

Library of Congress Control Number: 2021920056

CPSIA Code: PRV0923C
ISBN-13: 978-1-64543-937-0

Printed in the United States

To Old Souls and the Young at Heart

Why I Find You Irritating

Navigating Generational Friction at Work

Chris De Santis

with contributions from **Andrew Mortazavi** and **Tim McClure**

Contents

Foreword

"They (the youth) think they know everything and are always quite
sure about it."

Aristotle

In recent studies at the University of California to find the source
of what the researchers called the "kids these days" phenomenon, researchers asked adults about such things as authoritarian
tendencies, intelligence, and enthusiasm for reading. To no one's
surprise, they found that younger generations were judged by the
older ones to be "deficient on the traits in which they [the older]
happen to [believe they] excel." Specifically, the "authoritari-
ans" believed the members of the succeeding generation lacked
respect for authority, didn't read, and were, well, getting dumber.

What was interesting, these researchers concluded, was not
that successive generations are worse (or better) than preceding
ones but that succeeding generations may just suffer from a bad
memory. In fact, recent neuroscience research on human memory
has drawn the conclusion that our memories are far from static

and are heavily influenced by what is happening at the moment we remember something. According to Donna Bridge, a researcher specializing in human memory at the Northwestern University Feinberg School of Medicine, "If you remember something in the context of a new environment and time, or if you are even in a different mood, your memories might integrate the new information."

As the years stretch on for each us, it may just be that our memories of how things used to be when we were younger are simply invented realities, or at least not quite true to life. After all, it was not long ago that an entire generation came into sharp conflict with its elders over a foreign war.

A story from the *New York Times* recounts a Harvard commencement in which an alum exhorted the new graduates to support an evolving war far from our shores, saying: "We should consider it a duty and a privilege to fight for the safety of our country." He added that his generation of veterans "would be proud to see our boys go out there and do the job again."

Students responded by shouting, "Throw him out!" The commencement ended quickly. Booing drowned out the remainder of his speech as fistfights broke out. This was not a scene from the tumultuous sixties but from Harvard Class Day on June 19, 1940, shortly before the generation born in the 1920s, who became— upon reflection—the "Greatest Generation," and the speaker was a World War I veteran.

It is by no means the case that those who came before us are the only ones who can fall prey to generational distortions and biases. For those who lived long enough, the "arrogance of youth" can be just as debilitating. Recent results from the American Freshman Survey, an ongoing five-decade self-assessment survey of U.S. college freshman, found that over the past four decades there's been a dramatic rise in the number of students who describe themselves as being "above average" in academic ability, drive to achieve, mathematical ability, and self-confidence.

Yet actual performance across these areas has shown a decline from the time of the first survey in 1966. "Our culture used to encourage modesty and humility and not bragging about yourself," according to psychologist Jean Twenge, who led the analysis of the results. "It was considered a bad thing to be seen as conceited or full of yourself." One possible reason for this change in how young people see themselves is the fact that we live in an ever more connected world. With those connections comes the inevitable pressure to compare oneself to others. This pressure may, in turn, put pressure on us to turn inward—perhaps to an unhealthy degree.

Differences of any kind—whether they be race, religion, gender identity, point of view, or values—can make us or, if we let them, just as easily break us. But armed with an understanding of generational differences, we can work across generations rather than falling prey to the false notion that, as George Orwell wryly noted, "Each generation imagines itself to be more intelligent than the one that went before it and wiser than on that comes after it."

Whatever the ultimate causes of our differences and the resulting conflicts, it is possible to take a different path. Chris De Santis offers us a deeper and, importantly, practical understanding of just what these differences are and suggestions as to what to do to bridge them. Thus armed, we can overcome our differences—and perhaps even use them in ways that make this world better for every succeeding generation.

Mark De Santis
Entrepreneur

Setting the Scene

"Everything that irritates us about others can lead us to an understanding of ourselves."

C.G. Jung

In this book, we will dive deeper into the generational friction that drives misunderstandings. There is now a wealth of data on generational traits and theory that explains how generations take shape. There is also no scarcity of research, articles, and books on generational differences in the workplace. But my goal here is not to simply regurgitate what we already know. We shall instead look at how these differences inform our interactions in the workplace, thus the reason for this book's title—*Why I Find You Irritating*. Moreover, I want to explore how we might *better* interact. The tendency of more senior generations in positions of power is often to suppress the differences that younger workers exhibit. This instinct to enforce conformity on the young is not so much driven by a desire to repudiate who they are (well, at least not entirely), but rather by a desire to have them repeat the success they, the elder statesmen, achieved by doing what they did the way they did it. My strongly held belief, and reason for writing this book, is that we have more to gain by understanding and embracing the real and perceived differences between generations than we could achieve by wasting time and effort in getting others to conform to our ways of doing things.

We have better data on generations, better studies, more research, and a more sophisticated understanding of generational dynamics than ever before. However, we aren't using this understanding to actually embrace our differences. Even when boomers in leadership positions do understand generational differences, accommodating the differences of Gen Xers, millennials, or Gen Zers in the workplace is more the exception than the norm. Even Generation X managers who are simultaneously being squeezed from above by boomers in leadership fail to fully accommodate the younger generations. Instead, the older generations push back against these young whippersnappers (although this term most likely predates boomers by a generation or two) and their strange ways. Rather than embracing generational differences, they often try to break others of their "bad habits." As a society, we are saying, in effect, here is how you are wrong about who you are, and this is how you must be instead.

Humans are social creatures, and we want to belong, to be part of something larger than ourselves, but at the same time, society is moving away from conformity and embracing that which is unique and special about each of us as individuals. I don't see this issue as a paradox but rather an opportunity. In this book, I refer to accepting and embracing our uniqueness as lopsidedness. It is the recognition that we are each a collection of unique skills and traits, and when we are part of a team, it is better to have a group of individuals with unique contributions and perspectives than it is to have teams of people who are redundant to each other. Workplaces need to be designed in a way that reflects this new reality.

Many existing work processes such as feedback, teaming, and evaluation aren't congruent with this new reality and, at the same time, firms are squandering the potential value they could get out of leveraging generational diversity. What might be seen in the eyes of some as weaknesses or failings might actually be strengths when fully embraced.

My hope is that this book can help anyone in leadership better understand the workers that they lead and manage. This book may also help anyone responsible for important processes such as recruiting, evaluation, employee development, and/or rewards think more broadly as a consequence of understanding why we see the world the way we do. The workplace—and the world—would be better off if leaders recognized the differences and unique contributions of those they lead. As the cycle of generations continues to turn, effective leaders must strive to understand those who are entering the workplace, and they must be willing to redesign the work environment in a way that is both welcoming and accommodating without sacrifices to the mission and purpose of the organization. Yes, the generations of workers that follow and precede yours are different. But no, *different* is not bad. Differences broaden our perspectives by providing new insights. These are assets that should be embraced and harnessed. I am in no way suggesting this is easy. I'm a boomer, and while I understand and accept generational differences intellectually, emotionally my first reaction to some of these differences isn't always magnanimous. Like everyone, I am a work in progress. Some days it's two steps forward, others it's one step back, but difficult as this can be there is only one direction to go and that is forward.

When I talk about generations in this book, I am generally

talking about the commonly defined generational cohorts. Different experts have different start and end points for generations, but for our purposes, we will go with those put forward by the Pew Research Center[1]:

GENERATIONAL COHORT	BORN BETWEEN
Traditionalists	1928–1945
Baby Boomers	1946–1964
Generation X	1965–1980
Millennials	1981–1996
Gen Z	1997–2012

These cohort groups are constructs in that they can help us understand how people with opinions and worldviews fashioned by different times and circumstances interact with each other. These concepts can help us understand how people from very different generations interact. They help us interpret behavior and motivation. Generational labels allow us to better understand people as citizens, as family members, and, especially for the purposes of this book, as *colleagues*. This has a real and profound impact on our understanding of society, the economy, the home, the political sphere, and the workplace.

I have divided this book into two parts. The first part of the book looks at the how, what, and why of generational differences. The second part of the book examines how some work processes could be changed or enhanced to more fully leverage these differences and create a more humane and inclusive workplace. My suggestions, while focused on accommodating the needs and wants of

---

[1] "Generations Defined", Pew Research, March 1, 2018, https://www.pewresearch.org/st_18-02-27_generations_defined/

younger generations, regardless of their generational affinity.

A few words about our newest work cohorts, Gen Z, starting with their moniker—they have been called Gen Z and zoomers. These names have been assigned to them by various "experts," but they have yet to choose their own name. Millennials were originally called Generation Y, but the title didn't stick. I intended to use "zoomers" because it feels more distinctive than Generation Z or Gen Z, and the word zoom is both a product of our times in that Zoom calls have become a defining method of communication, much like millennials are associated with the landmark changing of the millennium. The second reason is the definition of the word—traveling quickly. I think they will want to quickly achieve things (a desire that is often mistakenly labeled by members of other generations as impatience).

Gen Z as a name doesn't seem very creative or unique, since we had Generation X and Generation Y (which they dumped). I did a search on Google Trends to see which term was most commonly searched for, and in spite of my preference for zoomers, Gen Z was the most searched of the two. That is why I have chosen to use Gen Z instead of my preferred choice, zoomer. Going forward, if we stick to the alphabet as the basis for the etymology of generational names, the children born after 2012 would be Generation A or Alpha. Ultimately, their names aren't my decision; they are theirs. If they end up with a different name before you read this, my apologies, it was just my best guess at the time.

I have included Gen Z in this book because they are present in the workplace. However, the challenge is there is very little data regarding how they are doing at work. They haven't made their presence felt—*yet*. They will. I had to be somewhat speculative regarding how they might engage with work based on how they were raised and what they experienced growing up. The problem with extrapolating into the future based on their collective experience doesn't account for how they will interact with other generations at work. The point being, they are a mystery yet to be solved, but I hope to provide a few clues as to what we might expect.

Now, a short public service announcement with regard to objectivity and bias. As I mentioned, I am a boomer. This was probably readily apparent from the photo on the dust jacket, though I would be greatly flattered if you mistook me for someone from a younger cohort. Though I am doing my best not to allow my own generational perspectives to bias my views, I am no less a product of my time and circumstance than anyone else. While I strive to see my own biases, I suspect some readers will be quick to note any of my missteps or blind spots. This is probably fair. While I will attempt to present an objective view, the boomer in me will make itself known from time to time. In the spirit of this book, please accept my apologies in advance. We are all, after all, only human, which makes us each uniquely imperfect.

Chapter one begins with an exploration of bias at work. We will see that our interpretation of a situation may conflict with how others see and interpret the same situation. Having contrary interpretations of the same event is referred to as a "Rashomon effect." Its name comes from the 1950 Japanese film *Rashomon* by the legendary director Akira Kurosawa. In the film, four witnesses to the same murder have very different interpretations of what happened. The difference in my story is that it takes place in a twenty-first-century corporate boardroom, and, thankfully, no one dies unless you consider embarrassment in the figurative sense.

Part One

The How, What, and Why of
Generational Dynamics

Chapter 1: The Rashomon Effect

"We don't see things as they are, we see them as we are."

Anaïs Nin

Zach stood looking at himself in the light-framed bathroom mirror. He had just gotten home from his job at a management consulting firm.

"What the hell happened?" he asked of no one in particular.

Retracing his steps over the last few days, Zach tried to piece together how such a promising day had gone so wrong. Bob, a senior partner at the firm, had invited him to an executive briefing with one of their longstanding clients. Zach was recently promoted to project manager and would be working on the account. The meeting was executive level. Normally, a mere manager wouldn't be invited, but Bob wanted to show him the ropes. Zach had a hunch that Bob was also grooming him for even better things at the firm.

"You don't need to prepare anything. Just come along and see how it's done," Bob had said. "Bring someone along to take minutes, and make sure your belt matches your shoes. Tomorrow, 2 p.m., at their offices."

Zach thanked Bob and returned to his office. He was excited to sit in on such an important meeting. He had been in the industry for a decade and with his current firm for several years. As a new manager, he was eager to show he could handle the added responsibility. Maybe he could even make partner someday. He could dream! But first, he needed to nail this meeting; he started to formulate a plan to do just that.

He had a good idea of who to bring along to take minutes. Becca, the summer intern, had just been hired full-time. She always showed initiative. Zach was certain she could handle the notes and that she would appreciate the opportunity. When he invited Becca to the meeting, she accepted the offer before he had even finished making it. Becca could do this, he was sure of it, and—even better—Bob was going to be impressed with his inspired choice.

Zach wanted them both to show up to the meeting prepared. In his new role, he had access to client billings and the proposed work-flow documents. He and Becca spent the afternoon reviewing the full client history and even did some online research. By the time they headed to the meeting the next day, they could have coauthored a book entitled *How to Stand Out in an Executive Briefing*.

The meeting was to take place in the boardroom at the client's headquarters, which happened to be only a few blocks from the office. Zach and Becca hoofed it there by foot, welcoming the chance to burn off some nervous energy. They showed up a few minutes early and waited outside. Bob was coming from another meeting and would meet them there.

The meeting was an alphabet soup of executives. The CEO,

the COO, the CFO, and the CIO—they were all seated in the latest ergonomically correct aluminum and leather executive chairs around two large parallel slabs of glossy walnut connected by three delicate butterfly joints. Zach was impressed, the table probably cost more than he and Becca make in a year. He plopped down in a chair next to Bob. So that she could hear everyone properly, Becca settled in near the center of the table next to Sarah, the CEO. Bob sorted some papers and cleared his throat, ready to kick things off. Zach locked eyes with Becca and they shared a quick smile. This was a golden opportunity. They were ready to show Bob he had made the right move bringing them along.

Bob gave a brief presentation on the project and the proposed overhaul. He outlined a plan to expand the team by adding two new roles. When Bob mentioned that Zach would fill one of these roles, the CEO furrowed her brow. Zach didn't like the look of that—did she have some objection to him? He had been working on the project for a few months now. Thankfully, Zach had done his homework and come prepared. He could show her he was the right person for the role.

"Sorry, can I just add something?" he interjected.

"What's that now?" Bob snapped.

Zach was taken aback by Bob's tone, but he ascribed it to the impatient nature so common among the senior partners. Normally, Zach would back down, but this was important. He needed to make his own case, lest the CEO pull him off the project. Only later would he realize that he had misread the situation and made a mistake. Unfortunately, this epiphany didn't come to him at the meeting. He thought it too important to prove himself. Zach went on to explain the new roles could be fulfilled collaboratively by the whole team. Siphoning that workload off into standalone positions probably wasn't necessary. Worse, an already-cohesive team might end up more fragmented. What the team *really* needed, in Zach's view, was a single full-time supervisor underneath him, the manager, to coordinate tasks.

Pleased with himself, Zach fell quiet. *Nailed it*, he thought. He looked to Bob for a little well-deserved validation of a job well done. Bob did not seem happy, though. Bob looked disgruntled. He was aggressively capping and uncapping his bespoke Montegrappa gold nibbed pen and scanning the faces of everyone else around the table, a worried look on his face.

A cold, heavy stone formed in Zach's stomach. Was Bob upset? Why? What had Zach done wrong? Was he not as clear as he thought he had been? They must have misunderstood him.

Before he could clarify or ask Bob his thoughts on the matter, Becca came to the rescue. She told a story about how, as an intern at another company during college, she had worked as a liaison and coordinator in a similar role. "I was really able to bring the team together working in that kind of role," she said in support of his idea. Zach was initially happy for the support, but unfortunately, as she continued speaking, it only seemed to make things worse. The entire C-suite was now trading impatient glances. The CEO glanced down at her wristwatch and then up at Bob. Her expression teetered between skepticism and commiseration, as if to say, *Who does this girl think she is?*

The longer Becca talked, the more annoyed the meeting participants became. Something had clearly been thrown off-balance: They either didn't like Becca's story or they didn't like Becca, which meant that they also wouldn't respect Zach's choice of Becca to play a role moving forward. Zach felt a little baffled; even befuddled. How could someone not like Becca? She was great.

Coming to her aid, Zach asked various members of the executive team questions about their own experiences with bringing a team together. Caught off guard, they fumbled awkwardly with responses. Seemingly oblivious to the situation she had created, Becca started responding to their offhanded replies. She would nod along in agreement. She would even shake her head and offer feedback. Zach held his breath every time she chimed in to offer advice on how they could handle things better. Even though Becca was making good points, Zach could see that it was upsetting Bob.

The rest of the meeting was a bit of a blur. Bob rushed through the final portion of his presentation before reclining into his ergonomically correct seat with an audible sigh of relief. The topic of discussion changed to another project. They had made it through. Taking their cue from Bob, Zach and Becca sat quietly and waited for the meeting to wrap up.

There had been some rocky points, but Zach felt mostly positive with how he had handled his first high-powered meeting. He clearly could have worded his contribution better, but it was still a good idea that seemed to have appeased the CEO.

While her contribution hadn't gone over so well at all, Becca did seem to salvage things at the end. As the meeting adjourned, the CFO asked Becca how she was making the adjustment from internship to her first "real" job. Becca being Becca, her response was quite frank. She shared not only what she liked about the new position, but also what she *didn't* like. She mentioned an idea for how she thought the firm could improve the onboarding process. She then asked the CEO how *they* handled onboarding and training at *their* company.

Zach was a little shocked by her frankness, but the CFO and even the CEO seemed to like her. *Maybe her story hadn't landed so poorly, after all,* Zach thought, now somewhat relieved. That was good news for him too, as her reception with the client would reflect upon his judgment in bringing her.

So, on balance, Zach left the boardroom with Becca and Bob generally feeling good about the meeting. Unfortunately, that feeling disappeared in a puff of smoke as the elevator's automatic doors closed behind the three of them.

"What the hell was that?" Bob snapped at Becca. "You're telling our clients how we can run our own firm better? Are you kidding me? We don't air our problems in front of clients. And it's not up to *you* to decide what is and isn't a problem."

He turned his ire on Zach next. "We don't have time for either of you to be talking over us during an executive meeting."

Zach tried to stammer out an apology, an explanation, *something*.

Bob didn't want to hear it. "You two were there to observe and learn, not to take over *my* meeting. You embarrassed yourselves."

What he didn't add, but Zach later realized to be true, was that they had embarrassed *him*, too.

Before getting off the elevator, Bob muttered, "I'm starting to believe what people say about you millennials."

He went on to lecture them about the meeting being a squandered opportunity to learn something. He said that he would never have acted that way when he was "their age," that no one would have. Zach started to tune out, as he always did when older people at the office started ranting about how it was "back in the day." He had heard hundreds of these stories, thousands even, and they were always just thinly veiled criticisms.

Zach was upset. He felt chided for merely having contributed. Once Bob got off the elevator to attend the next meeting with the client, Becca confided in Zach that she felt the same way.

"Give me a break," she said. "We went above and beyond. We did *more* than we had to do. And what do we get for it? Scolded like children? *Okay, boomer.*"

What could Zach do but nod in agreement? They had broken some unwritten rules that didn't even apply anymore. This wasn't 1975. Who cares what it was like back then? Not them.

"And he called me a millennial," Becca continued, laughing. "I'm too young to be a millennial. Not that he would know, he just thinks everyone younger than him is some dumb kid, even you!"

They felt justified in their feelings and happy to commiserate.

———

Later that day, Bob partook in a little collegial commiseration of his own. After his last meeting, he stopped by another senior partner's office. Bill was engaged with some documents at his desk, but Bob was sure he wouldn't mind the company, so he plopped down on Bill's austere Scandinavian modern leather sofa. Bob liked talking to Bill because, in his view, they "got" each other.

"You won't believe what just happened to me," Bob said.

"What's that?" Bill asked, looking up from his papers.

Bob told the story about the "kids" he brought to the big client meeting. "I just wanted to give them an opportunity to sit in and see how it's done. And they practically took over my meeting!"

"What did you do?" Bill asked.

"You know I don't suffer fools," Bob said. "I set them straight. How else are they going to learn?"

Bob and Bill went on to trade stories about other "insolent young employees" and colleagues. They concluded that the future was going to hell in a handbasket.

"What the hell is wrong with young people?" Bob asked, sincerely wanting to know.

He wasn't just venting. He really wanted to know.

——————

If there's a punch line to this story, it isn't funny. Bob, Zach, and Becca are all left feeling bitter and misunderstood. They aren't wrong to feel that way. They *do* misunderstand one another, and these misunderstandings have serious consequences in the workplace that can damage business relationships and firms. In this case, Bob has had his prejudices against young workers confirmed and might double down on screening out applicants that show what he perceives—largely incorrectly—to be disrespectful behavior or bad habits and traits. Zach always liked Bob, considering him endearingly "old school" but generally nice, but he now feels like Bob doesn't appreciate his contributions. Zach wonders if he still has a future with the firm. He's thirty-three now and has invested so many years there.

Poor Becca wonders if she even *wants* a future working for such a sanctimonious blowhard. She spends the night browsing job postings on LinkedIn over her second black cherry hard seltzer. She also contemplates all the bad things she is going to write about the company in her employee review of the firm on the company review site, Glassdoor. This isn't out of spite, not entirely. Young people today often measure companies and workplaces not just by their reputation in the marketplace, but also by how they treat their employees and how seriously they take their social and environmental responsibilities. She doesn't want to work for a company that is making the world worse or its employees miserable.

No one is happy. But it didn't have to be this way. They are each viewing the world from their generational perspectives and interpreting the actions of others through their differing generational lenses. They are misinterpreting one another's expectations, motivations, and behaviors. It could have gone differently if they made a genuine effort to understand each other well ahead of this important client meeting.

What Really Went Wrong

As a consultant, I have seen this kind of story play out again and again in the workplace. The setting and characters change, sometimes, it is a law firm or corporate headquarters, other times a small startup, or perhaps a mid-sized nonprofit. The dialogue varies. The cast rotates. Costumes include either suits, business casual, scrubs, or the jeans-and-tees free-for-all of the creative and tech industries.

What *never* changes in this narrative is the source of the dramatic tension. The conflict comes from the same wellspring of generational dynamics and related misunderstandings. Older generations in management and leadership find themselves in conflict with younger workers that behave in—what they consider—baffling and unprofessional ways.

The key to understanding these kinds of miscommunications between workers is realizing this is not necessarily a function of age. These misunderstandings usually arise from profound differences in generational interpretations of events that are a result of diverging perspectives. Younger workers are often misunderstood by their older Gen X managers and the boomers in the upper echelons of leadership. Boomers see less tenured workers acting in ways that they often attribute to immaturity or unprofessionalism. Unfortunately, Gen Xers are often required to act as intermediaries, sandwiched between those who manage them (boomers) and those they manage (millennials and Gen Zers).

In our hypothetical story, the senior partner (a boomer) misinterprets the motivations of his millennial and Gen Z colleagues. He interprets junior-level workers' contributions at an executive meeting as disrespectful and out of line. Boomers were taught to respect authority and hierarchy. They often fall back on the old adage of their youth: "children should be seen and not heard." Conversely, millennials and Gen Zers were raised to be actively inquisitive and engaged. Their genuine desire to contribute to the conversation is often read by older workers as self-serving or, worse, insubordinate. And no professional wants to be viewed as "a child."

Now, whether or not you agree with that summary (which, dear reader, will probably be a function of your own generation) is beside the point. Even if you tend to agree that the younger workers should defer more to management, it would still be a misreading of their intentions to ascribe their engagement as intentionally rude. They are trying to contribute in the way that they were taught. They were raised to be this way. These aren't necessarily bad qualities, as any boomer or Gen Xer would agree; but, in the workplace, older and experienced workers interpret this behavior negatively. In our scenario, the senior partner read Zach and Becca's actions as disrespectful. He was raised in a world where superiors and subordinates stayed in their own lanes. He was raised to defer to the boss and respect the established hierarchy. This is how boomers were taught to behave both at home and in the workplace. Conversely, millennials and Gen Zers were raised to be inquisitive and participative, which can be *incongruent* with how they are expected to behave at work.

Understanding these generational dynamics allows us space

for more genuine, productive, and cordial cooperation in the workplace. In a better world, our hypothetical story would have played out so that the senior partner would understand the motivations of his young charges. However, in the *best possible* world, the senior partner would have set up expectations of their roles in advance of the meeting. During the meeting, he would have listened thoughtfully to their contributions, asked relevant follow-up questions, and distinguished himself as a progressive leader in front of the client.

In turn, the younger colleagues would have understood where their boss was coming from, and they would not have been so quick to ascribe malice to his actions. They could have expressed their interest in contributing to the meeting and perhaps been given a more visible role. Remember, too, it is not always the case that older workers will manage and lead younger ones. The reverse of this ideal scenario is often the case. Getting the best out of people, regardless of their generation, requires understanding who they are, their impact on each other, and what they need to do their jobs well.

Chapter 2: Talkin' 'Bout My Generation

"Music, rock and roll music especially, is such a generational thing. Each generation must have their own music, I had my own in my generation, you have yours, everyone I know has their own generation."

Ronnie James Dio

Before discussing the four generational cohorts and their place in history, we must first begin with some caveats. Many people experience a knee-jerk reaction to any talk of generational traits and differences. They are quick to dismiss generational theory as, at best, pseudoscience cooked up by corporate marketing departments and academia and, at worst, online clickbait. This reaction is usually due to misperceptions about generational theory.

I can't blame the critics here. Generational theory often gets discussed in sloppy and inaccurate ways. Generational theory and legitimate studies on generational differences are regularly described anecdotally. This is true of all "soft" sciences. Everyone gets bad clickbait "psychology" articles in their feed on Twitter, LinkedIn, Facebook, or any of the alphabet soup of social media platforms—choose your poison. Still, we don't dismiss psychology. We condemn its pseudoscientific application.

Unfortunately, the soft sciences are easy to distort and misrepresent. They are a whole different beast than the "hard" sciences. The soft sciences deal with trends and generalities, not absolutes. Generational theory isn't physics or algebra. You cannot solve for X here. By definition, *everything* is a generalization. The trap some people fall into is thinking that generalizations are meaningless. They are not. Generalizations can be real, observable, probable, and quantifiable via statistical analysis.

In the case of generational theory, there is data and research to prove that the trends are real and the generalizations normative. To pretend otherwise is to deny one's own eyes and basic commonsense. No one can, with a straight face, deny that millennials are as culturally distinct from Gen X as Gen Xers are distinct from boomers. Arguing such a thing would be ridiculous on its face. No one seriously thinks that they grew up in the same world as their own grandmother. Boomers, Gen X, millennials, and now Gen Zers were raised in different times and so to some extent different worlds. Each generation lived through separate histories. They relied on different technologies. And each experienced different macroeconomic forces and global political environments. *Of course*, they are different. And if they are different, then generational differences are real. We are all products of both nature and nurture. This is the nurture aspect. How you are raised informs your behavior.

No one is arguing that boomers, Gen X, millennials, and Gen Zers exhibit the same behaviors, so how can someone understand this and still claim that generations are made up? The two beliefs would seem to preclude one another.

The answer: semantics.

We aren't using the same terms in the same ways to mean the same things. Many people that are quick to write off generational theory simply don't understand what we talk about when we talk about generations.

Before you start stereotyping, classifying, or pigeonholing others or yourself based on assumptions about age, consider these four important caveats:

1. Generational narratives are not destiny.
2. Generational narratives are neither global nor universal.
3. Generational narratives apply primarily to the American middle class.
4. Generational shifts are distinct from the "stages of life."

Caveat One: Generational Narratives Are Not Destiny

People often dismiss generational narratives when their own lives do not conform (or relate) to those narratives. They see generational trends as broad generalizations, easily dismissed. They aren't wrong on the first point, but the conclusion doesn't follow. When we speak of generations, we *are* generalizing. Since generations comprise millions upon millions of people, it should not be surprising to observe great variation among them.

People from the same generation are shaped by many of the same cultural, economic, and political *macro* forces, but they don't all react in the same way on a *micro* level. We all have our own genes, upbringings, personal histories, families, friends, and personalities. We lead our own unique lives, and it is not surprising that we do not make choices in lockstep with each other. The year we are born has an obvious bearing on our lived experience and how we were nurtured, but your character (as in, your nature) will always be more salient. Some people's lives just don't fit neatly into common generational narratives. But this in no way invalidates generational narratives. Your personal experience is anecdotal. As the saying goes, the plural of anecdote is not data.

The actual data doesn't lie, but our interpretation of it can be skewed. On average, compared to previous generations, today's millennials are earning less than previous generations did at the same age. They and Gen Xers are hopping jobs more than boomers did when they were their ages. They spend more time online and are more likely to get their news from the internet. Millennials are less likely to own a car or house. Millennials and Gen Zers are more educated and more in debt than either Generation X or boomers. Millennials are more likely to live inside urban centers as compared to those that came before (although many boomer "empty nesters" are now moving back from the suburbs into urban centers). Since the boomers, each new generation has been more liberal, more open to diversity, and generally more suspicious of unfettered capitalism. These tendencies aren't true for everyone, but they don't have to be. These are *tendencies*, not absolutes, and they are real in the aggregate. These tendencies are borne out by the data, whether your particular life conforms to them or not.

Insight can be gained from comparing and contrasting your life to your generational narratives. There has to actually be a grain in order to cut against it. People that defy generational narratives are often the exceptions that prove the rule. There are millennials and Gen Xers, however uncommon, that stay with the same company for years or decades. But this behavior is seen as curious by their peers precisely because it doesn't conform to expectations. Likewise, there are scrappy entrepreneurial freelance boomers, but they too defy society's expectations and may even face social scrutiny for their choices.

The existence of outliers, far from disproving generational narratives, actually shows just how thoroughly generational narratives define how people see us. You cannot defy generational trends without standing apart and risk being judged by your own cohort group. For better or worse, we are either defined by or against the generational narratives that people ascribe to us.

Caveat Two: Generational Narratives Are Neither Global Nor Universal

Some people criticize generational narratives for excluding the lived experience of many, even most, people around the world. The point is true, but not one to be ceded. When I speak of generational narratives, I am primarily, often exclusively, referring to Americans. This doesn't make generational narratives false. They are simply specific to the American experience.

Generational narratives about Americans should never be applied to people in other countries. Many more traditional cultures do not experience the rapid generational shifts that we do in the United States. William Strauss and Neil Howe, famous for their seminal 1991 book *Generations*, noted that individuals in traditional and orthodox cultures are usually permitted far less leeway to pursue their own identities.

This precludes the kind of cultural turnover we see in each generation in the United States, a nation founded on and rooted in rugged individualism. More traditional societies exhibit far less intergenerational variance. This is also true of more collectivist societies where there is less focus on individual identities. The less variance within society, the more limited the variance over time as well. China is a good modern example of both of these traits, being both collectivist and more orthodox than the United States despite the economic reforms that began in 1978. (However, a growing cohort of young, educated Chinese are exhibiting many of the same traits as American millennials and Gen Zers.) The children in the emergent middle classes in China, like their western counterparts, are being raised by parents deeply involved in their upbringing and to some extend are experiencing a global youth culture with the internet as its conduit. China's emergence onto the world stage in recent decades was a major shift that likely divides those who came of age on either side of it. I suspect the Chinese youth who are lucky enough to be the recipients of this economic and social leap forward are quite probably "chafing" under the pressure to conform to their parents' desires.

The United States is a particularly individualistic nation, but many other countries are rooted in the same individualistic culture that arose during the Enlightenment. These countries are mostly Western and share other values and norms with the United States. However, citizens of even these countries have had their own cultural, political, and economic environments that do not line up perfectly with the American experience. Generations are shaped by their shared experience. Their differing experiences have led to different generational narratives. Sometimes, there is overlap with American generations, but not always and not perfectly. We must be careful when applying our generational narratives to them even when we use the same generational terms.

For example, in the United Kingdom, the baby boom started slightly later and came in two waves, a concept I will expand upon in an upcoming chapter. American boomers were born approximately between 1946 and 1964, but the American baby boom actually started as early as 1939. People born that early are not actually boomers, but the baby boom was well underway and changing American life by the time the first "official" boomers came along. By comparison, the baby boom started slightly later in the United Kingdom and actually peaked in 1946, shortly after the war ended. While the United States was prospering in the post-war years, much of Europe and the United Kingdom immediately after the war were in the process of rebuilding their infrastructures and industries. The baby boom actually fell off and then resurfaced and peaked again in the early and mid-1960s. This created a British "boomer" demographic and experience that looked very different from the American one. There are obvious parallels, but we must be careful when generalizing across the two populations.

The caveat to the caveat here is that globalization continues to shrink and flatten the world. Culture crosses international boundaries with greater ease and speed. More people use online social media platforms, such as YouTube and Instagram, that allow them to view and learn from cultures across the globe. It's how K-Pop from Korea, Bollywood music from India, and Latin pop became global phenomena. English has become an international language in practice, not just theory, and cross-cultural international pollination is only accelerating. The term millennial has been applied elsewhere around the globe, particularly in Europe and Australia, but also in China and Japan. This didn't really happen with Gen X until after the fact and in a clear case of historical reinterpretation. Millennials are in many ways the first *global citizens*, competing in the same industries and for the same jobs, consuming much of the same media, informing themselves by a plethora of splintered made-to-fit sources, and developing something that is *just beginning* to look like an international culture.

Despite these trends, much of culture and economics is still local. It can be very tempting to think of young people the world over as the same, but they really are not. They may interact online, but in other areas of life, they have little if any interaction with people outside their home countries. They consume some of the same mass media as Americans, but not all of it and they also have their own news and entertainment. Nations still have their own cultures and subcultures. Economic cycles vary across the globe despite the integration of the global economy. It is far, *far* too soon to call the end of national cultures, which means that we must be careful when we apply American generational trends to other countries. One emerging trend could be the growing similarity among sets of informed, educated, urban cultures. All human beings may be shaped by some of the same forces, but they exert a very different push-and-pull in different locales. Where these forces don't align perfectly, neither will generations.

Consider also that the cultural specificity of generational narratives means that they will not readily fit immigrants now living in the United States. Depending on the country of origin and the circumstances of their arrival in the US, the children of some immigrants, even those with birthright citizenship, are less likely to identify with generational narratives than their peers. They are often raised differently than the dominant culture. The children of immigrants from many more traditional cultures are pushed to apply themselves and may be taught to obey authority, which cultivates traits and perspectives that are at odds with Gen X's distrust of authority or millennial assertiveness, for example. Conversely, the parents may be arriving from a country with an authoritarian or corrupt regime and as a consequence a distrust of authority in any form which would align with Gen X's distrust of authority. Immigrant populations do not fit well into generational narratives by birth years until their children or children's children fully assimilate into the dominant culture.

Caveat Three: Generational Narratives Apply Primarily to the American Middle Class

As I explained earlier, generations are shaped by shared experiences. Not all Americans share these experiences. Just as the children of immigrants are unlikely to participate fully in the dominant culture, the very poor and the very rich also have very different life experiences than the rest of the country.

Poverty locks people out of many cultural experiences and can preclude access to the same education, experiences, and even products that the middle class can more easily afford. Historically, poverty lessens the impact of economic cycles. Economic recessions have far less effect on communities already mired in intergenerational poverty. However, when coupled with other macro events (such as the COVID-19 pandemic) all strata are impacted. Impoverished communities experience few of the benefits of an expanding economy and less disappointment from economic contraction. Living through the Great Recession was a defining aspect of the millennial experience. Many college-educated millennials could not obtain the well-paying white-collar jobs they expected upon graduation. This is an experience not necessarily shared by those in impoverished communities where unemployment remained high before, during, and after the recession. Millennials growing up in poverty had it hard, but their dreams weren't dashed in the same way. Financial hardship has been a part of daily life going back generations.

Conversely, the very rich are typically insulated from the economic forces that shape generations, limiting the impact on their lived experience. The Great Recession affected everyone, but the cushion afforded by wealth softens the blow. The very rich also engage in cultural activities wholly inaccessible to anyone who isn't wealthy. They may still interact with many parts of the wider culture, but they do so from a place of unique privilege. This kind of privilege sets them apart from their peers.

The "latchkey kid" experience is a hallmark of early Gen X life, due to the expansion of women into the workplace and the increase in two-income households due to wage stagnation. However, there were no super-rich latchkey kids in the 1980s, even though this was a common childhood experience for Gen X. The very rich were seldom left home alone as their parents were less likely to work typical 9–5 jobs and help was easy to hire.

The class-specific nature of generations is another reminder that your lived experience trumps the year of your birth. If you don't share the same experiences as the wider culture, you are unlikely to conform to the generational narratives of that culture. Extreme wealth or poverty simply puts people outside of many of the cultural and economic trends that shape generations. The very rich and the very poor are still part of the dominant culture, but they lie so far on either side of the bell curve that generational traits and narratives are less likely to apply to them.

Caveat Four: Generational Shifts Are Distinct from the "Stages of Life"

When I give talks on how millennials are changing the workplace, invariably a boomer will raise a hand, squint askance at me, and say something along the lines of: "Won't they grow out of it?" The lilt of their voice pitches up at the end in exaggeration, which tells me that within their question is also a statement—a hidden assumption: "They're just young, *right*?"

The answer is *no*. No, this is not about millennials just being young. They are different, they always have been, and they always will be. The forces that shaped them, both economic and cultural, were different than the forces that shaped the questioner.

Older people sometimes fall into the trap of comparing younger people to themselves at that age. They see young people acting a certain way and deduce that they must be motivated by the same reasons that they once were. Millennials, as compared to boomers at that same age, are known to job hop. This is a generational trait that arose from precarious economic conditions and the dissolution of lifelong employment prospects. They know their employers aren't necessarily loyal to them and so they are not necessarily loyal to the employer. They will often commit fully to the employer in the short-term while being willing to hop companies for a slightly larger salary or small promotion in a way that young boomers were unlikely to do. That's because boomers grew up in a different world. Many of them worked for the same company their entire careers. They were led to believe that, if they just worked hard, they could have a job with the same company for their entire professional life. Many planned to retire with a pension. Boomers may objectively know that the workplace has changed, but still be puzzled by a young person's resume. If it shows multiple job changes, they are more likely to ascribe it to "flakiness" rather than "seeking better opportunities." They don't necessarily consider that the young person might just be exploratory, ambitious, and in search of more than just the elusive promise of a steady paycheck. They may also not consider the larger employment landscape of the times.

Boomers are not the first to behave in this way. As generations turn over, there is a tendency for the old guard to disparage the new kids on the block. Back in their day, the boomers were often stereotyped as hippies, potheads, or anti-war agitators that would rather smoke it up at Woodstock than make something of themselves. The members of Gen X were written off as flannel-wearing slackers that needed to wash and comb their hair. These complaints are often based on very real trends. Hippies were *real*. Grunge was an actual thing in the nineties. But these were just trends. Likewise, millennials are marrying later, more likely to live in cities, and more likely to purchase certain consumer luxuries like micro-brewed double dry-hopped IPAs.

However, these criticisms often take on a condescending undertone that brands the new generation as less-than-serious (much like the statement I made about their choice in beers). A byproduct of this thinking is that very real generational differences get dismissed as the passing foibles of youth. Surely you have seen the now-ten-year-long deluge of articles maligning millennials for killing everything from traditional marriage to the suburbs, mayonnaise, domestic beer, and even napkins.

While how we behave in our youth isn't always indicative of

how we will behave later in life, generational traits have been shown to persist as people age. Our worldviews are developed in childhood, which is why generational differences exist at all. We are shaped by our early adolescent years, and while we all grow and change, the lingering influence of our earliest perspectives and formative experiences never vanishes. Boomers were very different in their twenties and thirties than millennials are today. Millennials will not age into boomers. They will develop changing priorities with age, but not in the same way as boomers. The two cohorts were shaped by different economic and cultural forces. Much the same way that Gen Zers will not grow up to become like Gen Xers or millennials. Each generation is unique unto itself.

The research shows that generations retain traits. This is easily observed in political affiliation and positions. Surely you have heard this old saw: *If you aren't a liberal at twenty, you have no heart; if you aren't a conservative by forty, you have no brain.* Makes a good sound bite. Too bad it isn't true, at least not in the way you may think.

Research shows that people tend to remain affiliated with the same political party for their entire lives. The 1960 seminal study *The American Voter*[2] found that voters who came of age during FDR's New Deal were more likely to remain lifelong Democrats than those born shortly before or afterward. More recently, a study[3] on voting allegiance (conducted by Ethan Kaplan and Sharun Mukand) showed that registering to vote for the first time

---

2   Angus Campbell, Philip E. Converse, Warren E. Miller, Donald E. Stokes. *The American Voter.* Chicago, University of Chicago Press edition, 1976
3   Ethan Kaplan and Sharun Mukand, "The Persistence of Political Partisanship: Evidence from 9/11", February 2014, https://www.econ.umd.edu/publication/persistence-political-partisanship-evidence-911

in the month following the 9/11 terrorist attacks, was correlated with a higher likelihood of identifying as a Republican as compared to those who first registered only the month before. The most interesting finding of the study is that this effect *persisted for more than a decade*, the entire length of the study.

This casts doubt on the assumption that people grow more conservative as they age. Most people tend to hold similar political positions their entire lives. What changes, instead, is the world around them. Boomers hold many of the same positions they always have, but as social mores and attitudes change or evolve (depending on who you ask), boomers look increasingly conservative. But their views haven't changed. A 2014 paper[4] out of Columbia University shows how events in childhood and early adulthood imprint themselves on voters in ways that determine political voting patterns for the rest of their lives. Study after study has found similar findings.

Generational cohesion is not specific to politics—other traits appear to be sticky as well. Take something as common as news consumption. Obviously, millennials consume news differently than previous generations. They get the news on their phones and laptops, not from televisions or newspapers. However, they also spend less time consuming news according to the Pew Research News Consumption Survey[5] from 2004–2012 (as cited in the book, *The Next America* by Paul Taylor). Across the length of the survey, boomers spent an average of seventy-five minutes per day on the news whereas millennials spend only forty-four minutes. These are generational traits that are likely to persist

---

4 http://www.stat.columbia.edu/~gelman/research/unpublished/cohort_voting_20140605.pdf

5 Paul Taylor and the Pew Research Center, *The Next America* (New York: Public Affairs 2017) 43-44

over time. It seems, like political views, the time spent on getting our news remains consistent as a generation ages.

Perhaps the strongest evidence that generational shifts are not simply the result of an aging population moving through different life stages is that the different generations cannot even agree on the stages of life. Most boomers only recognize four major stages of life:

1. Childhood/adolescence
2. Young adulthood
3. Adulthood
4. Eldership

Each stage lasts roughly twenty years. When asked at what age they considered themselves adults, most boomers will answer "eighteen."

Millennials? Not so much. Most millennials see their twenties as an exploratory period between adolescence and adulthood. These are not young adults, but *emerging* adults, to borrow the language of Jeffrey Jensen Arnett from his book *Emerging Adulthood: The Winding Road from the Late Teens through the Twenties*, though the concept will be familiar to people whether or not they have read the book. *New York Times* columnist David Brooks has called these years the "odyssey phase." It is a time where young people discover themselves and who they will become, a luxury never afforded boomers and largely foreign to their life experience. The trend did not begin with millennials, though. Gen X generally believed adulthood started at the age of twenty-one or twenty-two, as they graduated college and entered the workforce. Millennials have just given themselves a couple more years to figure things out, perhaps due to a more precarious employment environment but also because they were raised to be exploratory by nature.

Going back even further to the time of the "silent generation" (also known as the "traditionalists" in either case, the generation preceding boomers), society was more rural and more middle-class people worked in the trades. Unskilled labor was common, and adulthood often started *before* eighteen. People were working on farms and responsible for the important duties and decisions as young as fourteen or fifteen. They contributed greatly to the family's financial base. They worked side jobs in their teens that might turn into actual lifelong careers. With just chores and schooling during the day and hardly any childhood diversions in the evenings, save for the family radio in the parlor, what else was there to do but want to become an adult? Their childhood as compared to my own boomer childhood didn't appear to be all that much fun.

By comparison, millennials are entering the workforce later than any previous generation, and they're exploring various careers before settling into a path. They move around more. They are delaying buying property and marriage. The average age of marriage in 1960 was about 20. Over the last 6 decades, the average age of marriage has increased to 27. For certain urban millennial populations, getting married before your 30 is considered downright strange.

The other big shift has occurred on the backend of life. The retirement age used to be 65. This is the age at which we become eligible for full Social Security benefits as determined when the program was instituted in 1935. Interestingly, according to the Social Security Administration, the average life span of all Americans at birth in the 1930s was 58 for men and 62 for women. However, lifespans have increased beyond our humble expectations. People are living longer, particularly those in the middle class. This trend may be changing due to widespread obesity, the opioid epidemic, the COVID-19 pandemic, and rising healthcare costs that have millennials and other Americans forgoing preventative care, all of which impact lifespan. Nonetheless, for now, this extra time in life has ushered in a new 6th stage of life, called bonus-eldership, people typically over 80 years old (or "dinner at 4 p.m. with a coupon").

These life stages are largely a product of generational changes, but not generational change itself. Confusion over this matter results in many intergenerational misunderstandings. Boomers expect people in their late twenties to have made all the major decisions of their life—what to study, whom to marry, what to do with one's working life—and when a young person hasn't done any (or all) of those things, boomers may think of them as lazy, immature, or irresponsible. For millennials, this is just normal life. Doing otherwise would be strange. They don't see themselves as those "adults" at twenty-five or even thirty, at least not in the same ways boomers defined it. They want to venture out, see the world, and try new things before settling down. It is because of millennials that "adulting" has become a verb and why "adulting classes" for millennials are on the rise. The distinction here is that boomers think young millennials are in an entirely different stage of life than millennials perceive themselves to be.

This is why acknowledging generational dynamics is so important, whether in the workplace or in regard to personal relationships. When older generations assume that generational differences are simply a result of age, we are likely to misinterpret those differences. We need to accept that we have moved from a four-stage model of life to a more nuanced six-stage model that includes the emerging adult and bonus elderhood. We have extended both adolescence and our senior years. The irony is boomers embrace this notion of resisting aging when it suits them (as in "sixty is the new fifty") but bridle at the millennial's "delay" in becoming an adult.

Chapter 3: Generational Waves

"We were a tribe—on one hand, invented, and on the other, no less real."

Ta-Nehisi Coates

L et's start this chapter with a definitive statement: *Generations are neither static nor well defined.* Generations are, to borrow the language of Jonathan Rauch of the Brookings Institution, "squishy concepts."[6] As we explored in the last chapter, generations are generalizations. Trying to shoehorn unique individuals into large cohorts creates thorny issues. The shoe doesn't always fit, so don't be a heel about this.

We also have to decide who gets which set of shoes. There isn't always consensus around when generations start and end. Is someone born in 1981 a millennial or Gen X? Depends on whom

---

6   https://worldin2019.economist.com/millennialsvboomers

you ask. The Pew Research Center says[7] yes, the millennial cohort includes children born between 1981 and 1996. As recently as 2015, the United States Census Bureau would have said no. While Pew has built some consensus around the matter in the last few years, it remains open to public debate. We only recently even decided on the *term* millennial. While Strauss and Howe coined the term in 1987, the earliest millennials were into adulthood before the term overtook the placeholder of "Generation Y."

Finally, is a generation, as many people describe it, really a "single pair of shoes?" Arguably, no. A generation is usually thought of as spanning 15 to 20 years. Across that span, the cohort group continues to evolve. No one would argue that someone born in 1981 is the same as someone born in 1996. In fact, someone born in 1981 is probably much more similar to a Gen Xer born in 1980 than a "fellow" millennial born in 1996. We group people into generational cohorts based on the belief that they share similar traits and lived experiences, but the reality is that lived experiences and the traits that they engender will change markedly over the span of a decade or two. I agree. However, I don't believe it invalidates "generational theory," nor does it disprove the existence of generations. Boomers and millennials are analytical constructs. This is not an exact science. But it is social science. Generational labels allow us to talk about people in terms of the forces that have shaped them.

That generations are a construct does *not* mean that they are not real. Constructs can be very real, even ones that try to map squishy concepts. Few would argue that the periodic table of elements or the biological taxonomy aren't real, but only one

---

7 "Generations Defined," Pew Research, March 1, 2018, https://www.pewresearch.org/st_18-02-27_generations_defined/

of them describes things in absolutes. The periodic table of elements deals with counting protons, neutrons, and electrons. That's a hard science. But the biological taxonomy that helps us understand where individual species fit into the kingdoms of life deals in far squishier concepts. Evolution is complex and twisting. Complex life is not easily shoehorned—to return to our previous metaphor—into categories. And yet, shoehorn we do. And as a result, we better understand life and evolution.

Generations may be "squishy" concepts, but they describe real qualities in people. The traits and trends are real. And they help us better understand our individual and collective places in modern human history. These constructs also exert an effect on how we view each other. When we say millennials are this way or boomers are that way, we are creating perceptions in our own minds. We are creating perceptions that become Pygmalion in the sense that they alter the way we treat each other and thus alter the way we engage and respond. Treat a person as you perceive a millennial to be and they're more likely to act in a manner that reflects your millennial expectations of them, a concept we will return to in detail later.

For now, suffice it to say that generational theory is real and useful, even necessary. We do ourselves no favors by doing away with generational theory simply because there are thorny issues to address, inconsistencies to smooth out, and caveats to issue and consider. People are different across time. Gen Zers are different from millennials. Millennials are different from Gen Xers. Gen Xers are different from boomers. Building models that help us understand the dynamics resulting from the differences aids our understanding of the world. We should not toss out generational theory. We simply need better, more accurate models of generational turnover.

What Are Generational Cohorts?

Much of the current understanding of generational theory can be traced back to German sociologist Karl Mannheim's essay "The Problem of Generations." Many have expanded on his ideas, but Mannheim laid down the basics and his understanding of generational cohorts has stood the test of time. He believed that generational cohorts were the result of rapid social and societal change that rendered each new generation distinct.

Generational cohorts are a relatively modern concept. Mannheim published "The Problem of Generations" in 1928. For most of human history, generational turnover was specific to individual families. Societal generations were not a matter of academic or public discussion at all until the latter half of the 19th century. The Industrial Revolution led to rapid technological and social change. While it started much earlier, the pace and the reach of these changes really started to expand at the end of the 19th century with increasing urbanization. By 1920, half of all Americans lived in cities and technology was advancing so quickly that—arguably for the first time in human history—people were now living in a world that looked fundamentally different from that of their parents. Societal generations were born.

There is a reason that generations are about twenty years long. Under the old "four stages of life" model we mentioned earlier, each stage was about twenty years long. Many people started having kids around twenty, which meant that familial generations turned over about every twenty years. Distinct societal generations do not form in the absence of societal change, though. Societal generations will not form when societal change doesn't outpace familial generations. Distinct societal generations only arise when the young grow up in conditions sufficiently different from those of their parents.

This is what creates generational traits that distinguish one generation from the next. The disparity between the lived conditions of parents and children is what makes societal generations of familial generations. Distinct societal generations simply don't form when your father and his father and his father all grow up in the Stone Age, or tilling the land for a feudal lord, or working the family farm that was passed down through generations. Societal change must outpace the raising of kids in order for distinct generational identities to form. People are less likely to see themselves as fundamentally different from their parents unless the world has changed sufficiently. While technological progress is not the only driver of societal change, it is a significant one that can have profound impacts.

One thing I believe Mannheim got partially wrong was his notion that not all eras would yield distinct generations. He believed rapid societal change was required to distinguish new generations from those that came before. In his day, there was no reason to believe that societal change would continue to occur so rapidly. The rapid acceleration of scientific discovery was new at the time. People were amazed at the pace of change. The first flight by the Wright brothers at Kitty Hawk (a mere twelve seconds!) had just happened twenty years before Mannheim was writing about generations. Humanity had come so far so fast, but it wasn't seen as a given that this rate of change would continue.

Of course, the exponential growth of technology has kept society evolving faster and faster. Every single familial generation in the last century has yielded another distinct societal generation. No American in the last century has lived in the same world as their parents. But Mannheim had no way of knowing that societal change would accelerate unabated over the coming century in all areas of industry and life.

Nonetheless, Mannheim got the basics right. Generational cohorts are the result of rapid societal change. Distinct generational cohorts arise when new generations grow up in a time distinctly different from those that came before. Familial generations give rise to societal generations when society changes faster than children become adults. When young people share a new and different life experience than their elders, they develop their own unique generational identity.

As a young boomer in college, when I needed to do research I would go to the library, find the references I needed, and then proceed to the room containing the microfiche. For those of you who aren't familiar with microfiche, it is a reel of indexed photographs of articles on film. I would find the reel I needed, load it in the machine and then search for the article of note. This was a tedious process that took hours. Today, this search can be done in seconds by "googling" it. Access to information is instantaneous. To some degree, the young may seem impatient when in fact they simply have different expectations around time (and everything else).

Younger cohorts have always been seen as different by their elders. And when there are substantial technological and economic shifts between generations, they *are* different. They came of age in a world different from that of their parents. As the old adage goes: People resemble their times more than they resemble their parents. We are the product of our eras.

How Cultural Catalysts Define Generations

The relationship between generations and time should come as no surprise—it's intuitive. Generations are inherently temporal. Generational theory is literally a taxonomy of people born across time. People are assigned generations based solely on the year of their birth. However, these groupings are not merely a result of chronological convenience. As I have said, societal generations arising from familial generations, which turn over continuously, we do not think of any 20-year period as a distinct generation. Societal generations as popularly understood refer only to specific ranges of time as, for example, Gen X being born between 1965 and 1981.

This creates some logical contradictions that we will get to in a moment. First, we need to understand how the generational cohorts that we do recognize came to exist. They are not merely the result of rapid change, which is constant, but also specific turning points, forks, and shifts in history.

Generations are shaped by our shared experiences—or, more precisely, our shared *memories*. Not all memories carry equal weight. Some events are so important that they create what psychologists Roger Brown and James Kulik famously called "flashbulb memories" in their seminal 1977 paper in the journal *Cognition*. Flashbulb memories stay with us forever because they capture a moment of great import or consequence. Some flashbulb memories are strictly personal—weddings, funerals, graduation, and moments of personal tragedy or great fortune can all create flashbulb memories. No one forgets the day they got married, got into a major car accident, or lost a parent. We remember these events until we die because they represent a pivotal time in our lives.

Other flashbulb memories are global or national in scope and are shared by many people. Most Americans remember where they were when the World Trade Center towers came crashing down. If you are old enough, you probably also still remember what you were doing when President John F. Kennedy was assassinated. If you've really been around the block a few times, you probably remember what you were doing when Pearl Harbor was bombed. Everyone remembers where they were, what they were doing, and how they felt when these things happened.

Generational theorists William Strauss and Neil Howe, who get plenty of ink in this book, would call such widely shared flashbulb memories "secular crises," as they are often negative or jarring changes that affect much, if not all, of the populace. I prefer to use the term "cultural catalysts," because these events need not be negative. The term, as I am applying it, is different than the way it is used in organizations as a means to drive positive change, though in some instances the broader definition would overlap. The moon landing in 1969 was a triumph, not a crisis, but it represented a major shift in how Americans thought of the present—and the future—of humanity. For the typical American, the fall of the Berlin Wall in 1989 was a positive cultural event that represented the triumph of liberalism and democracy over authoritarian communism. The ascendance of American hegemony and the end of the Cold War changed the way many Americans thought about our nation and its place in the world. These changes were long-term shifts decades in the making, but the image of the wall coming down was a cultural catalyst that captured the shift in a single moment. For these events to create flashbulb memories, you obviously had to be alive and old enough to be cognizant of them.

Secular crises and cultural catalysts are most impactful on the young. The young are more impressionable. Their minds are malleable; their worldviews are not yet set in stone. Secular crises aren't just memorable. They are *life-changing*. They get seared into the mind and merge with our worldviews. For the young, these events shape worldviews.

These flashbulb events are particularly powerful to the young. Millennials that watched the Twin Towers come down had their entire sense of the world turned upside-down. Until this moment, they were a sheltered generation. They were literally raised within the "bubble of love." It is not a clinical term, it's simply a term I use that refers to their parents' attentiveness to them, what author Annette Lareau would describe as "concerted cultivation." (Now that sounds like a clinical phrase.) Seeing America wounded so grievously on its own soil shattered the illusion of safety. It is one thing to experience the event that shatters the illusion of safety, but it is another to come of age post-illusion. Young Gen Zers grew up with code red drills at schools as an outcome of the proliferation of mass shootings. As the world turns and events unfold, they will continue to shape generational worldviews in cohort-specific ways.

This isn't to say that 9/11 was not a shock to Gen Xers or boomers, it was a traumatic and scarring event for many. But their worldviews were already shaped. They were much older at the time and their views were largely determined. The Vietnam War had a far more profound impact on the worldview of later-wave boomers and early Gen X kids than the War on Terror ever would. Events such as these affect all Americans, but they have a greater impact on young people in their formative years than older people with established perspectives and a firmly entrenched sense of identity. These events give rise to a sense of shared identity for budding generations. While the COVID-19 pandemic will have a profound effect on all of humanity, the pandemic will be most indelibly written into the DNA of Gen Z.

You need not be a literal child for these cultural catalysts to shape your worldview. While childhood is a formative period, we continue to develop our sense of self through adolescence and into young adulthood. How old you are when you experience cultural catalysts does impact how they affect you. This becomes relevant across a single generation because generations, as we already know, can span two decades.

Consider the millennials. The earliest millennials grew up in the "end of history" era of the 1990s, a time when it seemed as if the economic expansion would continue forever. It was the era of the dot-com boom, when billions of dollars were invested in start-ups with the hope that these enterprises would be the next big thing. Millennial children were raised on the very American belief that each generation does better than the last. This dream was dashed when the Great Recession derailed their careers. Some graduated right into the recession. Others saw burgeoning careers evaporate overnight. The data shows that, to this day, many of them have not wholly recovered financially.

These older millennials were not children when the financial crisis struck. However, their worldview was undeniably shaped by the economic crises. The collapse of the markets and the ensuing recession were among the greater cultural catalysts that defined their sense of identity. The Great Recession left an indelible mark on these early millennials. To be a millennial was to struggle in a newly destabilized economy in which the promise of American prosperity and permanent growth had faltered. Many of them were well into their mid-twenties when these events took place, but they still defined their lived experience.

Conversely, the millennials in the latter half of the generation *were* children when the Great Recession struck. Born as late as

1996, the youngest millennials weren't even in high school when the housing market collapsed and the stock market tanked. The worst of the recession was over by the time most of them entered the workforce. In fact, many graduated into the strongest American economy we have seen in decades. By the time millennials born in 1996 graduated college, unemployment rates had dropped to around 4 percent.

Nonetheless, the Great Recession still left an important mark on these millennials. They remember the economic turmoil of their early years. They saw parents lose jobs and homes. They had older siblings that struggled to launch, never leaving home, or doing so only to come back. Though young and not yet fully out in the "real world," they still internalized the anxiety and uncertainty of the era. Meanwhile, members of the Gen Z generation, still in their formative childhood years at the time, are likely to internalize this anxiety in an indirect but equally palpable way. They may not remember 9/11 or the Great Recession, but the anxiety of the times will leave its mark on their collective psyches and thus their worldview.

Cultural catalysts send shockwaves out into history. They are a loud *bang*, followed by waves and ripples that can be felt far into the future. The closer you are to the bang, and the younger you are, the stronger you feel the shockwaves. These cultural catalysts are powerful events. They don't just affect those that live through them. They can be just as impactful to those who come of age shortly afterward. The echo is heard as sure as the bang. The more profound the event is, the stronger the ripples, and the higher the waves.

This makes intuitive sense. History is nothing but a long, woven tapestry of traceable cause and effect. The events of 9/11 led to the War on Terror. The youngest millennials were five years old when the Twin Towers collapsed. They probably don't even remember it happening. They lack that flashbulb memory. Nonetheless, they lived through the War on Terror and internalized many of the feelings and anxieties that marked the era, just as they internalized the Great Recession. They may have only watched footage of the Twin Towers coming down well after the fact, but they lived through the aftermath. The world in which they grew up had changed irrevocably. This sudden shift left a mark on the era. It left a mark on them.

Cultural catalysts aren't always this profound. They are major events that send shockwaves out into history. But waves come in all sizes, big and small, and small waves still travel out and undulate as sure as larger waves. The oldest boomers here probably still remember The Beatles appearing on *The Ed Sullivan Show* for the first time in 1964. The last of the Baby Boomers were too young to have any recollection of the event. However, society remembered The Beatles playing *Ed Sullivan*. Younger boomers saw their siblings plaster Beatles posters up on bedroom walls. The Beatles becoming mainstream was a watershed cultural moment that ushered in the age of rock 'n' roll. This was a major cultural force that would separate boomers, young and old, from their parents. Was it as profound as the Vietnam War? No. But the rock 'n' roll phenomenon and hippie movement were profound, and, in many ways, closely intertwined.

The Problems of Generations: Generational Heterogeneity and Living on the Cusp

The disparity between the experience of early and late millennials is not unique to their generation. History does not advance to the next chapter neatly every twenty years. Change is ongoing. Major cultural catalysts can cause rapid change. Consider the fact that President George W. Bush's approval rating went from around 50 percent to over 90 percent after 9/11[8]. But these large secular crises are not the only drivers of cultural change. The fabric of history is a roiling sea of smaller cultural catalysts sending waves crashing into one another at all times. Generational waves, as I mentioned, come in all sizes, big and small.

No generation is static; our lived experience shifts as time marches forward. Boomers who came of age in the early 1950s remember Dwight D. Eisenhower in the White House and the beginning of the Cold War. They grew up watching *Father Knows Best* on black-and-white TVs and the "non-habit forming" and "healthful" calming effect of Chesterfield cigarettes. Many of them grew up in single-income families where the father held a good-paying job, perhaps, if you were white, secured through education paid for by the Servicemen's Readjustment Act of 1944, commonly referred to as the G.I. Bill. The Act did not specifically deny benefits to black servicemen, but their opportunity to get the benefits ranged from troublesome to impossible. Boomers who came of age in the late 1960s were able to tune in their color TVs to watch President Richard Nixon railing against communists from the Oval Office. They watched protests, riots, and scenes from the Vietnam War play out in their living rooms, in vivid color. Meanwhile, their much younger Gen X siblings couldn't tell the good guys from the bad guys, and thus they internalized these scenes much differently.

---

8 David Moore, "Bush Job Approval Highest in Gallup History" *Gallup*, September 24, 2001, https://news.gallup.com/poll/4924/bush-job-approval-highest-gallup-history.aspx

Taking an even more granular look at the boomers, we can observe the subset that came up in between these two bookends. These were people that came of age while President John F. Kennedy was in the White House. The Cuban Missile Crisis easily met the criteria of being a cultural catalyst. Well before that event—beginning in 1951—children were taught to "duck and cover" under their school desks in response to the threat of a nuclear attack by the Soviets. They grew up witnessing the advent of the civil rights movement. I recall watching TV as a child and recoiling at the sight of police turning loose dogs and fire hoses on Americans, young black men and women, who were risking their lives to protest segregation.

Early and late boomers lived fairly, even radically, different childhoods. And yet, we call all of them boomers. They share many of the same cultural experiences. They all grew up in post-war America. They all lived through the Cold War. Anti-communist rhetoric shaped their worldviews. They had their world transformed by broadcast television. Nonetheless, we cannot deny that someone born in the mid-1940s had a very different lived experience from someone born in the mid-1960s. They are as different as they are similar.

Early middle-class boomers grew up in a sanitized post-war America that was practically nostalgic in its own time. They were handed an idealized vision of America. While everyone didn't share equally in the American dream, middle-class Americans for whom the dominant cultural narrative was created, the myth of post-war America held great power even at the time. It was all Dinah Shore singing about seeing the USA in your Chevrolet riding across America on concrete ribbons, stopping at a Howard Johnson's for a lunch of fried clams, and staying overnight at the Holiday Inn with a built-in swimming pool. Could life be better than this? This cultural myth gave way in the 1960s and early 1970s as the civil rights movement and the Vietnam War brought chaos and upheaval to the country. These were turbulent times—and they happened right in the middle of the baby boomers' formative years. Late boomers were greatly affected by these changes. If boomers can be so different, what does it even mean to be a boomer and how is the label even useful?

This question brings us back to the apparent logical inconsistencies and deficiencies of generational theory that we touched on at the start of this chapter. The further apart two people are born, the less they are likely to share in common. This seems to support the notion of generations until you start looking at things at a granular level.

To truly understand the relationship between people and their times and why we sort them into generational cohorts as we do, we cannot look to greater granularity. We can only divide people into so many groups. We must instead develop a better model for understanding generational evolution and turnover.

For that, I offer the concept of generational waves.

Generational Waves

The contradictions of generational theory have been around as long as the field itself. These problems predate Mannheim's "The Problem of Generations," and they are solvable. The contradictions of generational theory arise from treating generations as homogenous static cohorts that turn over every twenty years or so. We need not toss out the notion of generations, which are ingrained in the actual culture and the American perception of itself, in order to stop thinking of generational cohorts in this rigid, absolutist way.

Generations are not static because the forces that shape them are dynamic. Generations are shaped by the ebb and flow of cultural, economic, and political forces. These forces are dynamic, which is why they shape generations differently over time. Cultural change is not always sudden. It is typically gradual and at times lurching. Generational cohorts are not, and have never been, discrete groups of people moving in lockstep until one January 1, when the old guard steps aside for the new. Generational turnover is much more fluid. Generations crest and break like waves. They crash and roll into one another.

The language of time is replete with water metaphors. We speak of time as a current, and that it is fluid, rippling outward. These metaphors capture the motion of time. They also capture the dynamic nature of generations, which are inextricably linked to time. This is why waves make an apt metaphor for generational turnover.

While the image of rolling waves might lend itself to the notion of cyclical motion, I do not ascribe to the belief that generations are cyclical. This is a key component of the Strauss-Howe generational theory. While I respect their work, I do not believe that generations are cyclical because history is not cyclical. Despite the old adage, history does *not* simply repeat, at least not in any ordered manner. History is idiosyncratic and disordered. Since historical events and trends are what shape generations, we should also not expect generations to be cyclic. History doesn't repeat, and neither do generations.

However, generational evolution can be undulating. Generations don't turnover so much as rise and fall like waves, driven by the rise and fall of powerful cultural and economic forces. These forces do swing back and forth. The markets go up and down. Progressivism leads to inevitable reactionary backlash. President Franklin D. Roosevelt clearly enacted the New Deal due to the crisis of the Great Depression. His expansion of the welfare state also led to pushback from conservatives. The current rise of both rightwing and leftwing populism is largely a response to economic inequality created by deregulation, austerity, and the rollback of the welfare state. But we can only draw a clean line from the Great Depression to the new populism of our current political era with the benefit of hindsight. Generational wave theory offers explanatory value, but little *predictive* value. No one could have predicted the exact nature of each wave in advance. History is far more complex than a simple pendulum.

Despite the lack of predictive value, generational wave theory does help us understand generational turnover more accurately. Thought of in this way, generational cohorts do not need to be divided and subdivided in order to account for *intra*-generational change. Generational cohorts, as largely understood among generational theorists, are large groups of people that have been shaped by a certain set of cultural catalysts. If we think about the effect that these catalysts exert as shockwaves moving through history, we can understand how people in different stages of life or under different circumstances will experience them differently. This helps us account for the variation that develops within each generation over time.

Generational wave theory allows us to understand these great intergenerational shifts, which drive generational turnover, while also accounting for the ongoing, unceasing *intra*-generational drift and variation that happens all of the time. Viewed this way, we can better understand generational cohorts as they rise and fall. We can make sense of the effect that these cultural catalysts, big and small, have on people as they send shockwaves rippling out through history.

A Brief Generational Timeline

Let's now take a quick look at the generational turnover of the last eighty years, through the lens of generational wave theory. We will discuss each generational cohort in far more detail later in this book, but for now, we'll just focus on the rise and fall of each generation as it emerges from the previous generation, crests, and rolls into the next. Note how cultural catalysts ignite change and how evolving macroeconomic conditions shape each generation. We will place special attention on economic conditions in order to track how major economic booms and collapses act as cultural catalysts.

The earliest boomers came of age in a time of unprecedented abundance. This was in stark contrast to the hard times that came before—the Great Depression, the Dustbowl, and the Second World War. The United States, which was spared the carnage that all but leveled Europe, emerged from the war as the dominant economic power of the world. New industries were popping up and flourishing. Factories that had been converted into wartime production facilities went back to making consumer goods. Blue-collar and white-collar jobs were plentiful and paid well. Things had never been better.

In a sense, the earliest boomers grew up alongside the United States. They were coming of age as the country was coming into its own. This era came to be known as the "Great Compression," as the benefits of economic growth were benefiting Americans of

all economic stripes, thus compressing a large part of the population into the middle class. Things felt good. The middle class
was growing. It seemed like everyone had a shot at the American
Dream. Never before was a generation raised on the belief that
hard work was all it took to own a home and a car or two. This
wasn't limited to the affluent. People of all stripes had a shot.
Prosperity, abundance, and triumph were what it meant to be an
American.

This unbridled optimism began to shift in the late '60s and
early '70s. The youngest boomers, in the second half of the
cohort, saw the economic expansion begin to crest and break.
Race riots broke out across the country. The Vietnam War was
drawing to an end, but it had left grievous scars upon the country.
The economy was cooling and the guarantee of a good job that
was so central to the identity of the boomers was already starting
to evaporate in their time. Things weren't that bad, but they felt
more tenuous than they had only a decade before. This second
group of boomers experienced the first taste of the rising forces
that would come to define Gen X.

By the time the earliest Gen Xers were coming of age, the
"covenant" had been fully broken. The "covenant" meaning if
you worked for a large company, and did what was expected,
you could retire from that same company with the promise of
a pension. The Great Compression ended in the mid-seventies
when corporations began "rightsizing" white-collar jobs right out
the door. Boomers grew up in a world where the average man
(yes, generally always a man) could hold a good job for life and
support a family on a single income. While younger boomers saw
this version of the American Dream begin to unravel, Gen X did
not have these dreams dashed. They never knew such a world.
They grew up with the understanding that jobs were not for life.

They grew up in a world in which nothing about your career or livelihood was guaranteed. Not everyone who worked hard would succeed.

They also grew up in a world in which the traditional social fabric had begun to unravel. Boomer children had witnessed subtle shifts in the autonomy of women. They saw their mothers as more independent and empowered in their marriages than their grandmothers. However, Gen X was raised in a brave new world in which women could work and lead lives (outside of the home) of their own. Not only could they, but they often *had* to. While there are obvious benefits to women gaining more equality and autonomy in the workplace, the shift had consequences for Gen X children. More households with working mothers meant that more kids were home alone.

Their mothers were not only gaining more autonomy at work, but they also gained more autonomy in every aspect of their lives. The divorce rates started to shoot up in the early 1960s with the increasing availability of no-fault divorces. According to a *Business Insider* article[9] reviewing divorces and divorce rates over the past 150 years, Americans saw divorces more than doubled from 1960 to 1975. These rising divorce rates and the prevalence of dual-income households gave us a generation of "latchkey kids"—those children were left at home for significant amounts of time after school before a working parent returned home. Personally, it is my belief that early members of Gen X replaced the economic anxiety that the previous generation had developed with the loneliness (and perhaps feelings of abandonment) as a

---

9   Frank Olito, "How the Divorce Rate has Changed over the Last 150 Years", *Business Insider*, January 30, 2019. https://www.insider.com/divorce-rate-changes-over-time-2019-1

result of absent parents. I suspect it is one of the reasons why as adults they are so engaged with their own children's lives.

The shifting economic cycle had just as profound an effect on Gen X as it did on the boomers. While boomers are generally associated with economic expansion and prosperity, the later boomers actually came of age in a time of growing economic uncertainty. Transitioning from economic growth to economic contraction was a major intra-generational shift. Gen X experienced the opposite shift. While Gen X evokes images of latchkey kids in the popular consciousness, the second half of the cohort came of age during the dot-com boom. President Bill Clinton was in the White House pushing a pro-growth economic platform. The economy was booming again. The stock market was up. Money was being made. The bubble was yet to burst, and people were getting fabulously wealthy off of companies that only really did well on paper—or, on a computer screen, as it were. This wealth trickled down throughout the economy.

Though this fortunate reversal in the economy had a great material effect on Gen X, the generation retained its general flavor. Gen Xers young and old were viewed by many as malcontents as in the rise of the "grunge" culture. They were portrayed as slackers and cynics. The image of the Gen X disaffected nihilist was cultivated in Bret Easton Ellis's novel *Less Than Zero*, a reference that may only resonate with Gen X readers. We saw this throughout the generation—youthful disaffection was on full display in both the punk scene of the eighties and the grunge scene of the early nineties, both thoroughly Gen X phenomena.

Millennials were also subjected to a major economic shift mid-generation. The first millennials came of age during the same economic boom of the late nineties and graduated into a good economy. Even the bursting of the dot-com bubble was only a minor setback, especially given that millennials were young and didn't hold much in assets. These were golden years where everyone still believed they could "get rich quick" in a booming tech-driven service economy. Millennials like Facebook founder Mark Zuckerberg became overnight billionaires in their early twenties. Millennials were raised to believe they could be anything. For a while, this seemed true.

Then everything changed. In 2006, the housing market began to decline from its soaring highs. The bubble had burst. The stock market soon collapsed. The financial crisis of 2008 not only sent stocks plummeting, but it also marked the end of easy credit. Many millennials were laid off and couldn't find work. The youngest millennials watched their parents lose jobs and homes. We were back to times of uncertainty so severe that they hadn't been seen in almost a hundred years.

This economic shift created the great contradiction of the millennial generation. On one hand, millennials were raised to believe that they could "be anything" if they worked hard enough, a very specific and idealized version of the American Dream that prided individuals on their uniqueness and its devotion to building self-esteem. This style of parenting was prevalent throughout the millennial generation, but it ran up hard against the Great Recession. Millennials suddenly saw that hard work wasn't always enough in the new gig economy. They realized that they couldn't all be anything. In the new economy, they often couldn't even be what their parents were—successful middle-class citizens with some degree of economic security. Instead, many millennials were forced to cobble together a living out of part-time and temporary jobs. Many went unemployed and underemployed. Many returned home as "boomerang kids."

The protracted downturn is one of the defining events of

the millennial generation, but it is worth noting that millennials did not all experience the Great Recession in the same way. The oldest millennials were already in their late twenties and becoming more established in their careers when the financial crisis struck. Of course, many of them lost their jobs and ended up having mortgages larger than the value of their homes, but many also managed to recover. This is perhaps part of why so many early millennials identify more with Gen X. Millennials who came later graduated into the Great Recession. They were hardest hit by a protracted economic downturn that stole some of their best working years and derailed careers before they even began. The stage of life that millennials were in at the time had a great impact on how they experienced the powerful cultural catalyst that was the Great Recession.

During this period, the earliest of Gen Z kids were just young enough to benefit from the economic prosperity of the dot-com boom that their parents enjoyed. However, the majority of their childhoods were marked by the dot-com bust and the Great Recession, which left far more indelible marks upon them. Late-wave Gen Zers coming of age now are experiencing the COVID-19 pandemic and all its economic and "remote schooling" repercussions, a cultural catalyst that will have a significant impact on how they see and interact with the world around them. Employability and security will be two of their mantras.

Recessions and economic booms are one type of cultural catalyst that profoundly impacted the evolution of generations over time. Economic conditions really highlight the wavelike nature of generational turnover because the economic cycles move in waves. Other cultural catalysts also move in waves. The civil rights movement was not a battle won overnight, or even within decades, but rather through fits and starts of progressivism met with reactionary backlash over many generations. Understanding generational evolution across time means understanding how these cultural and socioeconomic conditions have shaped each generation.

Time and time again we see these dynamic forces shaping generational evolution. We see not only how generations turnover, but also how they *evolve*. We can see how these forces elicit slow change *within* generations. I have always thought that there were two sets of millennials, which I would term pre- and post-Rubicon millennials. It alludes to resolutely becoming someone other than you were assumed to be. The term was borrowed from Julius Caesar and his army famously crossing the Rubicon River in 49 BC in an act that was considered a treasonous insurrection by the Roman Senate and an act of war. He had been instructed not to cross the river. By doing so, he was committed and there was no going back.

I believe that millennials crossed their own Rubicon, so to speak. The demarcation, as I see it, comes when one approaches thirty, which according to some is the definition of the age of the "new adult." Many older millennials can see "millennial-like traits" in younger millennials but fail to see them in themselves. This is, in my opinion, because the generation continued to evolve past them, and they no longer fully identified with the generation. And why would they? Millennials are reviled and dismissed in much of mainstream media, which they see as the providence of boomers. I suspect that every generation has this before-and-after split—their own Rubicon to cross. Historically, society tends to cast every new generation in a negative light when it comes of age. It is merely the millennials' turn in the hot seat. The earliest millennials are simply old enough to attempt to identify out of the latest generation by virtue of their age.

The last of the late-wave millennials are now washing into the next generation, Gen Zers. I suspect the harsh light of judgment will soon be turned on this budding generation as it has for each generation who preceded them. They are also likely to see evolution under changing conditions. No doubt, they will eventually have their own Rubicon to cross. The earliest of their generation are just now graduating from college. They were children during the financial crisis and are coming of age in an era of immensely unequal economic prosperity and immersed in the long tail of the COVID crises. Where the economy and culture move from here is unknowable. We can see that they are likely to grow up in an age of growing economic inequality. Millennials got more than just a taste of inequality, but Gen Z may quite possibly be getting the full dose. We will only know when we see how the next chapter of history unfolds.

Chapter 4: Why We Generalize

"Our categories are important. We cannot organize a social life, a political movement, or our individual identities and desires without them. The fact that categories invariably leak and can never contain all the relevant 'existing things' does not render them useless, only limited."

Gayle Rubin

I n his doctoral thesis, "Transformational Grammar," the late linguist and public intellectual Noam Chomsky, argued that people use what he termed "mental filters" to make sense of reality. He identified three filters through which we sift incoming information: deletion, distortion, and generalization.

According to Chomsky, we use "deletion" to winnow down incoming information. The brain filters out stimuli that it perceives isn't important. We don't even notice white noise, for example. Many short-term memories are deleted without being saved as long-term memories. We only preserve the important or memorable. We also tend to exclude information that doesn't conform to our preexisting biases and beliefs.

While deletion limits what we take in, "distortion" edits what we keep. We edit memories. They aren't what we actually experienced, but what we *think* we experienced. Our brains aren't camcorders. They are interpretative cognitive machines capable of creativity, adaptation, and context. Our memories are distortions of reality.

Chomsky's third filter is generalization. When generalizing, we use past experiences to make assumptions about present encounters. Our brains would struggle to make sense of the world if we had to process all the stimuli around us as if it were novel. Instead, we interpret experiences in the context of past experiences. A few observed examples allow us to construct general rules about what to expect from similar experiences going forward. This is a useful mental process . . . within limits. When we see a dog barking, we interpret the meaning of the bark automatically based on a past experience. We know what an angry bark means. It means we are about to be bitten, or at least chased!

All three filters factor into how we perceive others, but this chapter will focus on "generalization." Generalization, if we are not careful, can also lead to implicit bias and stereotyping. An example of an implicit bias is that we tend to be more favorable in our views of attractive people than we are of those we deem unattractive. Interestingly, when you further examine what makes one attractive, one of the characteristics we look for in others is facial symmetry. It becomes an associated trait of attractiveness that resides below the level of our consciousness (unless, of course, the asymmetry is grotesque in its proportions), thus it is an implicit bias. Building on Chomsky's work, Dr. Shelle Rose Charvet, in her book *Words That Change Minds*, wrote that "Generalization is about how we unconsciously generate rules, beliefs, and principles about what is true, untrue, possible, and impossible."[10] Essentially, generalization is how we navigate our way through the world.

These three filters are also not constant across time. They are shaped by the larger cultural context in which we operate. We all generalize—but *how* we each generalize is a function of the culture of the day, our backgrounds, our upbringing, and our own idiosyncratic personalities as well. Our generational moment, place of birth, and life circumstances shape how we interpret new information and experiences.

Furthermore, our impressions and decisions aren't always rational or consistent. Passing emotions and fleeting moods can influence how we react to someone or something. Experience also shapes how we respond to similar experiences in the future. In their book *The Power of Bad*, authors Roy Baumeister and John Tierney point out that negative emotions have an especially profound impact on how we see the world. This means that a negative interaction or event can have a strong effect on our perception of the world. Someone that is mugged by a vagrant is much more likely to suffer implicit bias against a person who fits the visual criteria of a vagrant.

This can have a major impact on how people from different generations view one another. People of different generations came of age under different sets of rules, beliefs, and principles. We are often baffled by the behavior of people whose actions don't conform to the world as we know it. This happens often when older generations begin viewing the young as different and sometimes strange.

---

10   Shelle Rose Charvet, *Words That Can Change Minds* (Dubuque: Kendall Hunt, 1997), 9.

Such differences often foster an "us versus them" dynamic between generations. This leads to people retreating into their own groups. Each group will see its own behaviors, norms, and beliefs as "correct." This means that we see other people—those who are different than us—as behaving incorrectly. Their different behaviors are often interpreted as problematic, whether or not they are problematic, simply by because they are different. This often leads us to ascribe mal intent where it does not exist. Ultimately, we begin to generalize "negative" behaviors—and our own view of what those behaviors say about others—onto whole groups.

Here is the trap of generalization. We cannot avoid making generalizations because it is how we interpret and make sense of the world around us. But we must do so carefully and mindfully. Otherwise, our perceptions of others will often be skewed, inaccurate, and/or false. This happens when we start making generalizations about entire generational cohorts.

Generational cohorts, as they exist in the popular imagination, are ultimately the collective public perception of groups of people born within specified timeframes. These perceptions may be appropriate at the level of the group, due to the shared circumstances when coming of age of those judging and those being judged. As I mentioned previously, generational cohorts are really just subcultures shaped by the time in which they came of age and then entered adulthood.

Each wave of a generation is associated with a specific youth culture because of this fact. Kids will always be kids, but those who grew up in different times were raised in different ways. We lived through different formative (and, indeed, transformative) events. We came from different worlds. Politics dealt with different concerns. Mores and values were different. Technology advances from one generation to the next. In combination, these differences cause each generation to develop different traits.

We come to see the world in very different ways than the generations that came before. And, generally speaking, we come to see and interpret the world through the same shared lens as those who grew up at the same time. This is exacerbated by each generation's desire to find its own unique "voice." We all want to claim our own place in the world. Each generation is, in some ways, a reaction to what came before. We see this in popular culture, such as fashion and music, but also in evolving mores, norms, and attitudes. One example of this cultural evolution is the growing acceptance of the LBGTQ community in each successive generation, a reaction to past bigotries.

My point: the perceptions we hold about generations are based in reality. We are all most impressionable in youth. We pick up preferences, proclivities, and traits within those early years that never leave us. My friend Leo Benvenuti said it best: "You are where you came from."

Consider the effect of technology on how we communicate. My fellow boomers and I grew up with telephones. Even today, my preferred method of remote communication is by phone. I will certainly send an email or text, but whenever I can, I pick up the phone and dial someone. Gen X is more likely to use email when appropriate, as they grew comfortable with this form of interaction. Millennials are known to prefer texting to placing calls. Most millennials don't even have a landline anymore, and the youngest *never* did. The youngest millennials and Gen Zers have started moving away from text toward erasable chat platforms, such as Snapchat.

Generational differences are real, not just the perception of them. However, perception does work to reinforce the trait.

Habits become normative with repetition. The more we engage in the habit, the more normative it becomes. The more normalized these habits become, the more people engage in them. In this way, reality and the perception of reality enter into a self-reinforcing feedback loop and become a principle by which we operate.

Of course, not *all* boomers prefer the phone. Many Gen Xers prefer text to email. Similarly, not all millennials are glued to their smartphones. And believe it or not, there are people in the Gen Z cohort that are not on Snapchat or FaceTime. This kind of variance is to be expected when generalizing about generations. We don't all have the same individual experience even within a generation. Not all families can afford the same tech. Even within the middle class, which is the primary subject of generational theory, there is great variation. Some young people may simply not like social media or screen time. Generalizing across an entire group is problematic when you start looking at individuals and expecting each individual to conform to generational narratives. Many will not.

However, when we are generalizing at the group level, we can talk about generations without having to worry about variances within the cohort. This is because generational traits are *trends*, not absolutes. As we have discussed in previous chapters, these trends are not invalidated by exceptions that "prove the rule." Not all millennials have to be tech-savvy or prefer urban environments for these general trends to be true. We can make generalized claims about cohorts that are not homogenous. As long as the trends hold at the group level, we can safely claim that the cohort generally exhibits the trend.

This ability to generalize only works in one direction, though. We can draw valid conclusions about a group based on the individuals within it, but we must be careful when drawing con- clusions about individuals based on the groups to which they belong. While generalizing about *cohorts* has validity, we can— and many people often do—get in trouble when applying those generalizations to individuals *within* the cohort.

Unfortunately, this happens all of the time and is one of the risks of misunderstanding data based on generational differ- ences. While we may know objectively that generational cohorts contain much variance, we do not always *behave* as if we do. People are apt to apply broad generalizations to individuals. Doing so ignores the fact that generalizations are not absolute. This is a trap because it can lead us to stereotype individuals based on cor- related trends, in this case, related to their age and generational background.

Stereotyping and Salience Bias

When we apply generalizations about a group of individuals within the group, we run the risk of stereotyping. While the term has negative connotations, and it is often associated with prej- udice or even racism, there is no one alive that has not engaged in stereotyping. We do it all the time, not just with age (which is directly related to generational cohorts) but also with other identity factors as well. This is not a problem specific to gener- ational theory or theorists. It's a byproduct of being human. We *all* do this. Stereotyping is inevitable and pervasive. It's also dam- aging and destructive. Stereotyping involves the assumption that a trend (that may or may not be real) within a group applies to every individual in the whole group.

Case in point: consider Florida. For most people, the Sunshine State conjures up images of Disney World, beaches, palm trees, and probably lots and lots of retirees. Florida is sometimes referred to as "God's waiting room," a reference to the perception of the state as a place where people go to retire . . . and, more grimly, to die. The operative word here is *perception*. The cultural narrative about Florida is that retirees move there in droves.

There is more than a kernel of truth to the narrative. According to a *Business Insider* article published in 2018[11], the median age of Florida residents in 2018 was forty-two, one of the highest of any state in the nation and the highest of the larger states. However, despite the relatively advanced median age, there are many young people in Florida. We just don't *think* of them when we think of Florida. The cultural narrative about the state involves seniors, not the young (setting aside the temporary influx of Spring Breakers). When we think of Florida, we think of people going slow in the fast lane with a permanently flashing left turn signal and writing letters to the editor of the local newspaper claiming the world is going to hell in a handbasket.

There are two things going on here: one, the *reality* of Florida (in which there are many seniors), and two, the *perception* of Florida (in which we believe there are *even more* seniors than there actually are). The perception is based on the reality. There *is* an above average number of seniors in the state. However, the perception is often a magnified version of reality due to the before mentioned *salience bias*, which is a natural human tendency to notice prominent details and features. Observations become salient precisely because they are unusual. It has also been called

---

[11] https://www.businessinsider.com/state-median-age-map-2018-11

the "Tesla effect." This states that if you were to own a Tesla you would start to notice more Teslas on the road because of your heightened awareness of that battery-operated brand.

Salience bias reinforces and further exaggerates noticeable traits. We mistakenly take subjective, often anecdotal, information and misconstrue it as objective fact. In the case of Florida, the presence of lots of seniors can trigger us to start noticing older people. When people are primed to believe that the population is older than average, we have our beliefs further confirmed every time we spot a senior. Pretty soon, we are noticing seniors *everywhere*.

The salience bias shapes how we see everything, including generational differences. Generational differences are noteworthy—or salient—precisely because they are differences. Older generations, who did not grow up with technology, notice that millennials seem at home with computers. Boomers would not take note of this fact if they, too, had grown up with personal computers, the internet, and social media. Boomers only notice that millennials are naturally tech-savvy because they themselves are generally not—if they were, there wouldn't be anything to notice! Generational differences are thus inherently salient because they are what differentiate generations from one another.

The salience bias is self-reinforcing. When boomers repeatedly observe millennials rapidly adopting new technology, they start to take note and associate the trait with the group. The trait becomes more noticeable each time we see it. And after a while, we become conditioned to look for it in younger people. Eventually, with enough reinforcement, older cohorts start to *expect* this trait in millennials. They begin to assume that millennials are always adept at technology. I am not immune to this. When something goes wrong with my computer at work, I turn to the youngest people in the office to help me figure out the problem. They might know something about computers . . . but they also might not.

This happens not only on an individual level but also at the societal level. The trait eventually gains traction with the wider public. Soon, everyone "just knows" that millennials are good with technology, just as they know that only seniors move to Florida. If we're not careful, these traits become magnified as part of the cultural narrative. They feature in sitcoms and pop up in movies. They become the material of late-night TV jokes and internet memes. Perception becomes reality.

This is where salience bias can get us into trouble. Making generalizations about populations is a normal process, as in making sweeping comments about "Parisians" or "the French" or broader still, "the Europeans." Applying those generalizations to individuals is stereotyping even if when stereotypes are true about many members of a group, they are often not true for any given individual. Not all millennials grew up using the latest tech any more than the entire population of Florida is geriatric. Generations are not homogenous. We can only generalize about group norms, not individuals within the groups—not with any certainty or accuracy, anyway.

To Better Know Others, Know Yourself

Unfortunately, we often *do* draw inferences about individuals based on group affiliations. The human brain is wired to work this way. We make sense of the world through association and categorization. When meeting new people, we automatically place them into categories based on salient features, such as age, which roughly correlates with a generational cohort (unless, of course, they've had a lot of work done). This allows us to quickly draw all kinds of conclusions about new people based on limited information. This is sometimes referred to as "thin-slicing," whereby we make a quick appraisal of the person before us and arrive at a few hasty conclusions. The observer believes the conclusions are more likely to be right than wrong. That *may* be so, but they are still often wrong.

We cannot avoid this behavior, as it is simply how the mind operates, nor should we condone it, but we can mitigate it. Rather than trying to struggle against salience bias, the best course of action is to *manage* it by being more reflective and challenging your assumptions about others before you act on them. This is a two-fold process. First, be aware of salience bias and how you might be stereotyping people. Second, if you find that you do hold stereotypes of any group, ask yourself why that might be. Since we all make assumptions about others based upon generalizations, we need to understand the basis for the generalizations we make. There is no other way to overcome them. Those that are false can be discarded. Those that are rooted in truth can be used as heuristics for understanding differences, which are not necessarily bad, but merely differences. It's okay to use generalizations as long as we do so carefully and thoughtfully.

I am forced to generalize about audiences with whom I will be interacting. I test my assumptions in advance by asking who is in the audience, what issues they have relative to the topic, and their general attitude toward the topic. Doing this reduces my assumptions about them. While speaking, I reduce my salience bias by scanning the entire room rather than just attending to only a few people who are displaying favorable or unfavorable expressions.

Discussing generational *differences* is, by itself, an exercise in generalizations, but it is one in which we must engage. People are living longer than ever. Those of us who avoid an early demise are all going to end up sharing this planet with as many as six or seven, possibly even eight, other generational cohorts during our lives. Understanding how we are different from one another will only help us get along better. Understanding generational differences allows us to better interpret each other's motivations and experiences. We should not simply ignore what we know about groups or how it might apply to the individuals within them. Instead, we should be mindful of how we are generalizing and what assumptions we are making about someone based on their generation. Each generation and, more importantly, each individual is unique in his or her own way. While we may enter an exchange with others possessed of assumptions about them, the only **truth** is what we know to be true about ourselves, anything else is fodder for conversation.

This is extremely important for anyone managing or leading people in the workplace. We need to be aware of the biases we hold of others because they can lead to misperceptions. Our tendency toward misconceptions about others is what first interested me in generational theory. The entire point of this book is to help people avoid these misunderstandings, particularly in the workplace.

We all come to every human exchange with assumptions about each other. The better we understand those assumptions, the better we are able to understand each other. Knowing one's own biases and assumptions allows us to appreciate and celebrate our differences and avoid miscommunications. When you are aware of your own assumptions and biases, you are better positioned to avoid making unproven generalizations about individuals based on the groups to which they belong (or that you have placed them in).

The irony is not lost on me that I am suggesting we accept generalizing in service of reducing it or ameliorating its negative effects. But, given that we are all only human, that is what we must do. Generalizing is what we do. If we are not vigilant stereotyping is inevitable . . . but it need not dictate our actions toward others.

I prefer that we think in terms of heuristics—the application of commonsense in the everyday—as the term is neutral. While we can accept that we use heuristics to navigate the day-to-day workplace experience, we should never presume that our assumptions are necessarily (or always) *correct*. We cannot know another person's intentions or thoughts. The only thing we can ever be sure (and not always even then) is ourselves. Our assumptions about others are hypotheses that must be subjected to further inquiry and verification.

Talk to people. Get to know them. Make your assumptions, but make sure to verify them. This allows us some hope of eliminating our flagrant stereotyping of others. It's also a chance to get to know people who are different from ourselves so that we can learn to appreciate and embrace those differences.

The salience bias is based on our observation of the world. We notice generational differences and traits because they are real for many. Understanding our own perceptions about these differences also allows us to better understand and appreciate that we have more in common than we have differences between us.

As we will see in the next chapter, better understanding of other generations allows us to better understand the people within them. When we make unexamined and uninformed assumptions about other people, we are more likely to misrepresent their intent. For example, a boomer that gets a text message from their millennial direct report might find the action gauche and inappropriately informal. However, some millennials actually believe that phone calls are intrusive and overly intimate. By understanding this difference, boomer managers can avoid misconstruing their employees' actions.

This book is not just an attempt to help people understand other generations. I also want to help readers understand how their own place in history shapes their biases and assumptions. These things inform your view of others and others' views of us. When we understand our differences—both how I am *me* and *you* are *you*—we are better able to see how we are all simply different, again, not necessarily better, or worse, just different. When we can see and appreciate those differences, we are better able to work with others more effectively. We can see them more clearly, and they, in turn, can see and understand us more fully. As managers and leaders, you want your employees to understand where you are coming from, but first, you have to understand them— and ensure that you're not *mis*understanding them.

Chapter 5:
Existing (In)Congruence

"What one deserves and what one experiences are seldom congruent."

Jim Butcher

Intergenerational misperceptions are the result of having different vantage points. We typically generalize about others and apply our heuristics when they are observably different than us. We can only interpret others from our own perspective, which is informed by our own lived experiences. Since generational cohorts have shared life experiences, people in the same generation will share many of the same misperceptions of other generations.

It is a sad tragedy of the human condition that we so often fail to understand different perspectives. People from one generation often cannot understand how other generations experience the world. This is especially acute in the workplace. The modern workplace was mostly designed by traditionalists and then populated by boomers, who now hold many of the most senior positions in organizations. Recent generations have had to learn to function in a workplace that wasn't designed with them in mind. They find themselves out of sync with their environment. This places recent generations in a state of incongruence with their work environment. Boomers and the earliest of Generation X have not experienced this level of incongruence and simply don't understand it.

Incongruence with one's environment is rarely comfortable, especially when you are judged for it. I have always chafed against the way some people treat nonnative English speakers—as if they are slow or stupid. Picking up a second language is hard. Despite living in Madrid for a year, I never became fluent in Spanish. My Spanish was so bad that the locals would often switch over to speaking English with me. This spared them the horror of me butchering their language. While it often made me feel inadequate to have my language competency called into question, I was quietly grateful. Unfortunately, this mode of communication didn't help me learn the language.

My example is benign and easy to appreciate, but it pales in comparison to what many minorities and immigrants experience on a daily basis in the United States. Many nonnative English speakers find themselves in the same situation, but many Americans are unable or unwilling to offer the same accommodations. All too often, we simply treat people poorly for not knowing the language. This is negative stereotyping at its worst. Being the recipient of this treatment on a regular basis feels like death by a thousand cuts. It is its own form of microaggression.

What does language have to do with generational differences? Both can leave you feeling out of flux with those around you if you don't sync up. The language barrier prevented me from ever feeling at home in Madrid. Language is just one of the many cultural differences between Chicagoans and Madrileños, but it is a significant one. Language barriers obstruct the exchange of ideas and can create massive miscommunications. The locals knew I was a foreigner the moment I opened my mouth. They could hear it in the way I spoke. They couldn't *not* hear it. It was blatantly obvious. There are all kinds of everyday Spanish phrases that, slightly mangled, can easily become nonsensical or even lewd. I was always bungling common phrases. This inability to communicate effectively made me feel incongruent with the environment the entire time I was in Spain.

The same kind of miscommunication and disconnect can occur across generational lines when two people from different generations aren't "speaking the same language," so to speak (pun intended). Yes, we may all be speaking English, but all too often we don't realize what we are communicating to each other. When we come from different cultures—be that of different nationalities, or different generations—much can be lost in translation.

While we don't usually think of people from different generations as being of different cultures, in a sense they are. Individuals from different generations came of age in different youth cultures, with different tech, and under different political and economic conditions. They were raised with different values and mores. Generations really form under different communal life experiences. They are, in effect, *temporal* based cultures. Generational cohorts are, by definition products of their time. This is especially true given the accelerating rate of technological and societal change.

What happens when new generations live in a world created by the previous generation? A state of incongruence for the new generations that are forced to play by the previous generation's rules.

Nowhere do we see this more clearly than in the workplace.

Boomers still hold many of the top leadership positions. This will change in the coming years, as more boomers age out of the workforce, which will have profound implications. But, presently, boomers still run many organizations the way they always have, the only way they have ever known: as a hierarchical, "command and control" structure that defers to authority and seniority. They experience the workplace as congruent with their own lives and experiences.

Many Gen Xers, millennials, and now, Gen Zers do not experience the workplace in this way. They are often working in organizations that cater and adhere to a boomer sensibility. The workplace may have the sheen of a modern progressive air about it, but the underlying model remains the same. We've just moved around the furniture. This leaves many younger people feeling unhappy, disconnected, and frustrated because they find their work lives incongruent with their own sensibilities and world-views. While some organizations under younger leadership, most notably the tech sector, have embraced open offices, flex schedules, and more worker autonomy in order to cater to younger workers, most organizations still operate under a traditional corporate hierarchy in which most decisions are made at the top and handed down to workers.

I will not mince words: in the average office, boomers have it easier. They experience the workplace from a place of congruence with the rest of their lives. The workplace was fashioned in their image (or, more precisely, in the image of traditionalists, from whom the boomers adopted their conception of work and the workplace without realizing that an alternative was possible). As I will explain, it is why boomer leadership needs to embrace and listen to each generation as they enter the workforce and adapt the workplace and work processes to meet changing wants and needs.

The Vanishing Supremacy of the Tell-Do World

When I say that boomers find the average workplace in congruence with their lives, I mean that the hierarchy and command structure of the average organization resembles the authority structures boomers have known their whole lives.

Consider the boomer childhood. We were raised in what I refer to as a "Tell-Do" household. Instructions came from the top in a command-and-control parenting style. The parents were the commanders; the children were the subordinates. As children, we were told by our parents what to do and we listened. When our parents said jump, we asked how high. There wasn't any debate to be had. Failing to comply would result in unpleasant repercussions. "Wait till your father gets home" was the most dreaded string of words in the English language.

This was an authority model of parenting. It was always clear who was in charge. School was the same way. Instead of parents issuing orders, it was simply the teachers and administrators, but, in both cases, the hierarchy was clear, and orders came from the top. Once again, failure to comply and "behave" would result in certain (and swift) negative consequences.

There was no debate, no arguing with a teacher. The teacher was always right. When there were dustups or disagreements, we boomer kids were always wrong. We knew that our parents would always side with the teacher, no matter how wronged we may have felt. When the teacher sent a note home to our parents, we would be called into the living room and told to explain ourselves. Except this was merely a turn of phrase. Our parents didn't really want us to *explain* ourselves. They wanted us to acknowledge our transgression against authority and accept our punishment willingly.

The overall environment was more reliant on authority and showing respect for it. This concept existed not only in the family, but across all institutions. Although the profound social movements of the late sixties and early seventies started to challenge the role of authority, boomers were still raised in households where parents believed in the institutions of the time (i.e., church, governments, corporations).

Eventually, we boomers grew up and moved into the workplace. We experienced much the same in our first entry-level positions. Our first bosses treated us not so dissimilarly from how our parents had. They issued orders, and we followed. If you were a rare bird that, when given a directive, deigned to ask why, you were almost certainly greeted with the same non-reason that you had been hearing since childhood: "Because I said so."

The boomer experience, in terms of how we relate to authority, has been one of congruence throughout our entire lives. Our first bosses weren't any different from our teachers or parents. In the immortal words of The Who: *Meet the new boss, same as the old boss.* Granted, while the dynamic of our lives hasn't always been pleasant, it has been consistent. We have always understood that there is a pecking order and, generally, the world made our place in the hierarchy abundantly clear.

Eventually, for some of us, we moved up the career ladder and our roles and responsibilities changed. Some of us found ourselves in the boss's chair. We were now calling the shots, but it wasn't the structural and organizational *hierarchy* that had changed, just our place in it. We knew how to behave as bosses because we had already witnessed similar behavior from our bosses as we moved up the corporate ladder. We felt comfortable in these leadership roles because they were congruent with what we had observed in those who came before.

This has not been the experience of the successive generations. The pace of change in the workplace has not kept up with the parallel evolutions in parenting and education. More recent generations have had early life experiences that are increasingly incongruent with the Tell-Do workplace that boomers inherited and now head up.

Enter Gen X and the Suggest-Do Model

Gen X grew up in a markedly different environment than boomers. Boomers were raised under the Tell-Do model of parenting in which kids received and followed direct orders from their parents. Not so for Gen X. Changing economic and social conditions gave them, our first latchkey children, a much longer leash. More and more women were entering the workplace and taking on full-time employment, which meant that children spent more time home alone. There often wasn't anyone around to issue direct orders. These conditions mean that Gen X learned to be independent by necessity.

This independence resulted in some leveling of the top-down authority model. The Tell-Do model of parenting gave way to more of a Suggest-Do model. Gen X was raised by busy working parents that couldn't always watch over their children at all hours. Between school dismissal and the parents getting home from work, Gen X spent many hours home alone. Their parents were forced to trust them to make many choices on their own. Rather than issuing orders for and about everything, these parents would often *suggest* what their children should do. Rather than telling their children to do their laundry, they might suggest that they'll need something clean to wear to school tomorrow. And if the parents were on a roll, they might even suggest that their children clean their rooms before they got home.

While these might sometimes be *strong* suggestions that might eventually result in repercussions if not heeded, children knew that their parents had a more limited ability to enforce the rules when they weren't around. It was also easier for busy parents to simply allow their children to manage the small details of their own lives. This dynamic instilled Gen X with a spirit of self-sufficiency. They grew up to be more independent, cautious of strangers, and somewhat more skeptical of authority. These children were often referred to as "free rangers," as coined by Lenore Skenazy, a New York columnist, in a 2008 article in *The Washington Post* titled, "I let my 9-year-old ride the subway alone. I got labeled the world's worst mom." They were the last children in America to have a private life and to roam and play where and with whom they chose.

Meanwhile, as parenting was changing, so too were school systems. Authoritarian schoolmarms became a thing of the past. Instruction became more facilitative. Teachers began taking cues from social science research that suggested that students learned best when they were more fully engaged in the learning process. Schools began to encourage more inquiry from students. This further cemented Gen X's sense of independence and self-reliance.

Schools were not the only thing changing for young Gen X. Society as a whole had become skeptical of authority. Late-wave boomers and young Generation Xers experienced this sea of change. President Richard Nixon's fall from grace disillusioned many people and eroded their trust in authority figures. On the television, Gen X grew up watching Americans of all stripes protesting the Vietnam War and marching for universal civil rights. Young people were challenging the government, demanding change, and pushing back against the powers that be. This cultural shift embedded itself into Gen X, which to this day acknowledges and tolerates authority. They have internalized the Suggest-Do mindset, in which they are willing to hear out and even respect authority figures, but will ultimately draw their own conclusions, make their own decisions, and forge their own way.

This mindset led Gen X to create new youth subcultures, communities, and creative expressions that defied authority. An entire generation was questioning what they had been told about life and work. Their whole life, they had been given suggestions that they were allowed to question. They questioned that which had been *suggested* to them about the world. Many of them adopted "slacker" lifestyles, which while typically dismissed as mere laziness by older cohorts, were really the active embrace of skepticism about the state of the economy, the American dream, and the role of work in life.

Faced with a rude awakening that the secure and well-paying jobs enjoyed by boomers were becoming rare, Gen Xers felt the full brunt of emerging cutthroat global competition in the labor market. As a consequence, they had two options in the workplace. The first was acceptance. They could simply "go along to get along" and do as they were told. This left many of them deeply unhappy, which is part of why work employee engagement and productivity (which we will discuss in the next chapter) continued to plummet.

The second option available to Gen X was to start their own businesses and become their own bosses. Many, in fact, went this route. Opportunity in technology abounded. Many of those in the first wave of Gen X came up with the rise of the personal computer and the second wave entered the workforce in time to capitalize on the dot-com boom. Many Gen Xers with technical skills started technology companies, among other business pursuits.

Ultimately, Gen X muddled through work lives that were largely incongruent with their personal histories and expectations. This incongruence left some of them disillusioned and unhappy, but they are of a fiercely independent generational cohort that does well when left to its own devices. Just as they had learned how to make it home from school and entertain and feed themselves. They learned to navigate the workplace. Eventually, they figured out how to live in incongruence. If this is the world, so be it. Despite being maligned as slackers, they rolled up their sleeves, figured it out, and, in turn, got by.

This is one of the reasons that so little attention was paid to Gen X in the literature on generational differences prior to the arrival of millennials. Since their generational waves rarely rocked the boat; they simply flew below the radar.

Millennials, the Engage-Discuss Paradigm, and Workplace Incongruence

While Gen X found the dominant Tell-Do workplace model somewhat incongruent with how they had previously moved through the world, the millennial experience was far more jarring. The gap between how millennials were raised and how they are treated by boomers (who see them merely as subordinates) and by Gen X (who see them as needy subordinates) in the workplace is a wide and spanning chasm. Dear reader, if you recall the interpretations by Zach and Bob of each other's behaviors at the beginning of this book, you will have a sense of the gap that exists between these generations.

Once again, this incongruence can be traced back to millennials' formative years. Childhood experiences shape how we see the world for the rest of our lives. While Gen X was raised to be more independent, millennials were brought up under a whole new paradigm of "Engage-Discuss" in which parenting became more facilitative than it had ever been before. So far, this trend has largely continued with Gen Z as they have grown up and come of age.

Let me share with you a story that sums up how we have chosen to engage our young. I live in a pleasant neighborhood on Chicago's north side. The streets are lined with trees and children are allowed to play out on the sidewalk when supervised by an adult. It's the kind of place where you get to know your neighbors. I was sitting on my neighbors' porch one day when their two children came tumbling out of the house. Ben, who was six at the time, was crying and holding an iPad with a busted screen. His older sister, Stella, eight, followed close behind him. They are both late-wave Gen Z kids and, obviously, still quite young.

"He broke it, he broke it," Stella chanted to all present.

"What happened?" their mother asked calmly.

Staring down at the spider web of shattered glass in his hands, Ben proclaimed, "It broke!"

This much was obvious.

"How did it break?" his mom pressed, engaged but not angry.

She had to tease the story out of him. Eventually, Ben admitted that the tablet hadn't just broken on its own. Frustrated with a video game, he had punched the screen in anger, and it fell to the floor shattered.

If Ben were a young boomer, his mother would have probably scolded him. If he were from Gen X, his parents might have dismissed his crying with a "tough luck" pat on the back and reminded him that they'd told him to be careful with things. That's not what happened here. Instead, his mother engaged him calmly and asked a series of questions. Why had he been so angry? Was destroying his own things a good way to handle his anger? Had breaking the screen accomplished anything or only made things worse? She asked him what they should do now. When Ben said he wanted her to fix the iPad, she explained that the tablet would need a new screen, which was very expensive. She asked him whether he thought he had any obligation to contribute to replacing the screen since he had broken it.

I confess that, as a boomer, this exchange made me cringe. After about thirty minutes of listening to young Ben whine, I was waiting for the adult in the room to set this little kid straight. The authoritarian in me wanted him held accountable. I wanted there to be some repercussions for his actions! *Why wasn't anyone going to seriously reprimand this kid?*

None of that happened. Instead, I watched as Ben and his mother talked the situation through and came to a common understanding. Ben acknowledged that he was at fault and promised to control his anger in the future. They even settled on a positive, productive course of action. His mother would pay to have the iPad fixed, but as a way to contribute, Ben would start helping pick up around the house, not just his room.

As a boomer, I had never experienced this kind of parenting firsthand. My parents would have told me, "Tough luck, we worked hard to pay for your 'toys,' and if you can't take care of them, that's your problem!" That seemed like how things *should* have been, as that was all I had ever known. Upon reflection, it was clear that there were merits to the way Ben's mother handled the situation. The problem was discussed and addressed so that Ben understood precisely what he had done wrong. They now had a suitable plan of action to address the situation—and they had come up with it together.

This is what I call the Engage-Discuss model. While it does not call for an abolishment of hierarchy, this model of interaction involves open communication between the authority figure and the subordinate. Rather than harnessing punishment and guilt to change behavior, the authority figure (in this case, the parent) enters into an open dialogue with the subordinate (in this case, Ben, the child) and discusses corrective behavior. Ben's mother exemplified this model by engaging her son in open dialogue rather than defaulting to punishment.

This model hinges on a mutually established understanding that can only be achieved when the authority figure eschews coercion for open dialogue. When problems arise, the authority figure must exhibit flexibility, openness, and grace, and should avoid being judgmental. Whenever possible, they must offer the subordinate the benefit of the doubt and the assumption of good intent. The goal is to engage the subordinate in decision-making that results in a personal commitment to a new kind of behavior. The goal isn't simple compliance, but active engagement and collaboration that results in the commitment to new behaviors.

This cannot work when orders are issued without explanation. Authority figures must be willing to explain their reasoning in order to engage in dialogue. Under this paradigm, "because I said so" is never a valid reason for anything. The authority figure must actually engage the subordinate. They must explain why something is being done a certain way rather than simply issuing orders. In this new model, the subordinate is actively invited into a conversation about decision-making and the next steps. Ideally, engaging the subordinate in the decision-making process in this way makes them more invested in the outcome.

The Engage-Discuss model is not limited to parenting. Millennials operated under the same paradigm at school as well. Over the last few decades, the education system has shifted from a facilitative teaching model to a far more collaborative mode of teaching. Gen X saw the beginning of this shift, but as more and more school systems have adopted the new model, it became the primary way that millennials were educated.

Under the new education model, schools became more focused on collaborative learning, in which students work together to understand the material. Students were no longer seen as passive receptacles for knowledge handed down from the teacher. They became active participants in their own education. Less classroom time was spent on lectures and more was reserved for class discussion. Millennial students were regularly asked to "break into small groups" to work through material collaboratively while the teacher would roam the room and act as a guide, facilitator, and resident sage.

Taking a cue from social science research about various student "learning styles" (e.g., visual learners versus auditory learners, etc.), the newly emerging education system began to tailor education to individual students. Pedagogy began to place emphasis on the individual and their particular needs. This, in many ways, democratized the school system and allowed students a say in how they were being taught. Students provided feedback that helped establish methods and coursework in conjunction with teachers in order to come to an individualized education plan that catered to their own needs.

While this education model has been shown to improve learning outcomes, you can probably guess how millennials schooled this way fared upon entering the stubbornly Tell-Do modern workplace. In brief: not well.

Millennials found the labor market and contemporary workplaces even more incongruent with their young lives than Gen X had. Millennials grew up having a say in how they accomplished tasks and even what tasks needed to be accomplished. Inevitably, they were in for a rude awakening upon entering a workplace that had little interest in such open dialogue. Their bosses, mostly boomers and older Gen Xers, were accustomed to issuing orders and having them carried out without question. They had little interest in their young workers' opinions and even less interest in engaging in two-way discussions about policies and protocols. Suddenly denied the seat at the table to which they were accustomed, many millennials became frustrated with their employers and disengaged at work.

Their bosses, irritated with millennial workers' frustrations, were also not pleased. Boomers simply don't understand why their young workers are so upset. How could they? Boomers have never experienced the kind of incongruence that many millennials feel upon entering the workplace. Boomers grew up with the Tell-Do mode from birth. It is the only way they have ever interacted with the world. They are flummoxed by young workers that want to set the terms of their own employment or to have a say in how the company functions on day one. Older workers simply don't understand the suffocating incongruence that many millennials feel at work.

To boomers, the boss is the authority figure, and they call the shots—no questions asked, certainly not from some entry-level worker. Who are these kids that think they can question company policies and protocols? Boomers are outraged. They would never have acted this way as young people. They would have felt lucky to have the job and grateful for the opportunity. Who are these "kids" to act so entitled?

The great irony, of course, is that these "kids" are *their* children. It was the boomers (and the first wave of Generation X) that raised millennials to think and act this way. Millennials are often shocked by the way their bosses speak to them. They may not always say so, but they are resentful when their bosses "flip out" and throw fits for merely being asked questions or offered helpful suggestions. Again, recall the experiences of "Zach" and "Becca" in the opening chapter of this book. They were having a very visceral incongruent experience after the meeting in the boardroom.

These poor millennials don't get it. They are in culture shock. They know their parents would never have acted this way—and, of course, they are right. Their *specific* boomer parents did not treat them this way. That is the entire source of millennials' frustrations here. Their parents raised them to engage in open dialogue that does not interest their bosses. Ironically, it is these same parents that, collectively, are the bosses of this generation of millennial workers. If these same parents as bosses engaged their young employees in a similar manner as to how they engage with their own children, then there would be a marked reduction in the frustrations often felt by millennials and Gen Zers at work.

Boomers rarely acknowledge this paradox. They have compartmentalized their family and work lives. They see young people at work as younger versions of themselves that haven't yet put in the time and risen up the ranks. They don't see younger workers as colleagues or as *potential* equals, and they treat them accordingly. The irony! Remember, it is boomers that implemented the new Engage-Discuss paradigm at home. Most have just failed to make the intuitive leap that there might be some benefit in treating employees the same way that they treated their own children.

The data suggest there is tremendous benefit in adopting the Engage-Discuss model in the workplace. According to William Strauss and Neil Howe in their book *Millennials Rising,* published in 2000, millennials have experienced a decrease in crime rates, alcohol, and drug abuse, and exhibit a greater sense of responsibility to others and the environment as compared to previous generational cohorts. This model of parenting works and makes great citizens of children. Boomers and Gen X raised engaging and giving young people, a cohort that works well collaboratively and knows how to manage their own contributions; and yet boomers nonetheless rule over them with an authoritarian micro-management style. They expect these capable, collaborative, curious workers to conform to a top-down authoritarian management style that flies in the face of who they are. This is the very source of the uncomfortable incongruence that millennials feel at work. In a way, boomers set millennials up just to knock them down. This is not intentional. We boomers are not an evil cabal out to disenfranchise millennials. We simply see them as we *were* in the workplace and treat them accordingly.

Boomers also often misinterpret the millennial tendency to job hop as a lack of loyalty. They don't understand that this is really the result of two related forces. First, we now have a transactional workplace model that the boomers ushered in by breaking the worker-employer covenant (as we will explore in later chapters). Secondly, millennials are a generation in search of purpose, which puts them on a different kind of career path, which we will also discuss in later chapters. More relevant to the discussion here, millennials fail to grasp that it is the Tell-Do model of management that boomers impose on them that is making them unhappy. Boomers are quick to simply dismiss millennials as disloyal, lazy, or insubordinate, rather than to recognize and address the problematic work conditions that they themselves are creating. When workers aren't treated in a way that matches their needs and expectations, they will not offer their loyalty. The best employers can hope for, in cases like this, is compliance, which never lasts long in a transactional employment model.

Everyone loses when workers' needs are not being met. The young workers are frustrated and unengaged. Their bosses are perpetually annoyed and outraged. Everyone assumes the worst, which only further fuels negative stereotypes of "the other." Productivity falls and turnover rises. The business or organization suffers. Morale declines. The workforce remains disengaged. Ultimately, it is all of society that pays the price.

But it doesn't have to be this way.

The first step toward solving this problem is for senior leaders and managers to recognize that younger workers are simply *different*. Moreover, they must be willing to embrace, rather than attempt to stifle, these differences. Boomers *do* understand the merits of engagement and open discussion. They instilled these values in their children. Now they just need to embrace it in their workers. Figuratively speaking, in the collective, their children and their workers are the same people.

Boomers would benefit by trying to understand the "language" of millennials. They should remember how they raised their own children. They should offer them the benefit of the doubt and assume good intent. They should engage workers in open dialogue in order to come up with solutions and ways of operating that work for *everyone*.

Boomers and Gen X must stop incorrectly interpreting

millennials' contributions and engagement as insubordination. Millennials raised in an Engage-Discuss world are accustomed to participating in workplace dialogue. They believe that being on a team necessarily means having a voice in how that team operates. They believe (as do I) that they possess valuable insights that should be given a voice. Their boomer and Gen X bosses aren't used to this kind of engagement in the workplace from those that report to them. They are accustomed to issuing orders with the expectation that those orders will be carried out without question. But that isn't how younger workers operate, and it would behoove leadership to meet their younger workers in open dialogue. Do this, and we will be closer to a world in which we are all speaking the same language at work.

Leaders and managers are not abdicating their decision-making prerogatives by engaging in open, healthy dialogue. They are simply being open-minded and inclusive in how they operate and why they make the decisions that they do. Engaging in dialogue with reports and employees does *not* mean that management and leadership must accept all suggestions and cave to every demand their employees make. They need only hear them out and make an honest attempt at mutual understanding and reasonable accommodation, as appropriate. And, once boomers and Gen Xers are speaking the same language as their millennial and Gen Z workers, they will be better positioned to explain their own needs and expectations. We will all be better positioned to bridge this cultural divide.

Chapter 6: Work without a Net

"The real safety net of life is community, family, and nature."
Bryant McGill

One of the most powerful drivers of generational change over the last century has been the erosion of the covenant between workers and employers. Under this covenant, workers believed that companies would take care of them for their entire lives, and companies rewarded loyal workers by doing so. The breaking of the covenant led to the emergence of a more transactional labor market that changed everything forever. No other factor, save for technological change, comes anywhere close.

This change was experienced differently across the generations and left an indelible mark on each. Boomers were shaped by the promise (and erosion) of the covenant, Gen Xers by its disappearance, and millennials and Gen Zers by its absence. How they do or don't relate to the covenant is directly related to how they relate to the economy and to the emerging labor markets.

The covenant arose in the early twentieth century as a byproduct of the wartime economy and ushered in the era of the "company man." The company man worked for the same company for basically his entire career and expected it to take care of him in retirement. (I use male pronouns intentionally when referencing the company man. The company man was almost always a *he*, as women were yet to enter the professional ranks of the workplace in great numbers.) The demise of the covenant, caused by greater global competition, transitioning from manufacturing into services, and negative jolts to the economy in the form of stagflation ushered in a whole new economic order that would radically transform the American economy, workplace, and labor markets.

Workers could no longer depend on employers' largess, nor employers on their workers' loyalty. Career trajectories and advancement changed. Employers began hiring into positions that were once only open to internal candidates and promotions were suddenly less about seniority and more about competency. Workers were forced to hone different skill sets. The workplace—and workers—would never be the same after this implicit pact was broken.

The Rise and Fall of the Command-and-Control Economy

The American economy has gone through multiple transformations over the last century. While the upward economic trajectory of the United States can be traced back to at least the nineteenth century, the country did not emerge as an economic superpower until after the world wars. The wars required a massive mobilization of American industry. Tens of millions of American workers were directly or indirectly put to work in support of the war machine, especially once the United States officially entered the Second World War in 1941. Not everyone was conscripted directly into the military. Many men and women were employed as factory workers. American industry was retooled and ramped up, ready, willing, and eager to do its part.

This was a national mobilization of unprecedented scale that required a system of hierarchy capable of managing massive industrial production. The factories were effectively an extension of the military and were run as such. The manufacturing sector leveraged a top-down hierarchy to coordinate the orderly production of arms, munitions, and other military apparatus in accordance with the military's needs. American industry during this time was almost entirely geared toward the wartime production, and as such, was managed under a regimented command-and-control structure. This hierarchy allowed the federal government and military leaders to coordinate, and to some extent, even direct, private industry's role in the wider war effort.

This was such a massive industrial undertaking that it can be viewed as a second industrial revolution. The war eventually came to a close, but the industrial machine remained in place. While much of Europe and Japan had been leveled by intense bombing, the relative isolation of the United States and its late entrance in the Second World War meant that American factories were still operating. The country now had a veritable citizen army of manufacturers and skilled tradesmen. With the war over, these factories and workers went from making arms and munitions to producing consumer goods. The country stopped pumping out bullets and tanks and instead began cranking out cars, home appliances, building materials, and every consumer good imaginable.

Years of wartime rationing created a sudden demand for goods that had been scarce for so long. In a time when significant parts of industrialized European and Pacific nations were dealing with the aftermath of the war, post-war American industry ballooned in order to meet this new demand. Fully half of the world's manufacturing was happening in the United States.

This post-war economy gave birth to the aforementioned "company man," a phenomenon that transcended the manufacturing sector. The company man, whether he worked on an assembly line or in the office, was expected to develop a specific set of skills for a specific role within the company. In exchange, the company man expected stability, benefits, and protection from his employer for his entire career. *This* was the essence of the covenant. Workers remained loyal to companies and developed skill sets that matched their employer's needs. Companies took care of them during their careers and after they retired in the form of a pension. This was a symbiotic relationship. The economy was exploding, companies were thriving, and workers grew and advanced along with their own companies.

Corporate culture was very hierarchical, as you would expect in a command-and-control economy. Workers stayed in their lane and stayed the course, no matter what. This covenant bred loyalty between worker and employer, but the structure and culture of big companies were rigid and inflexible. The work environment was standardized and predictable. Career trajectories were set in stone. Company men moved in lockstep through their days and their careers. Specific roles in a company required specific skill sets. Growth within the company involved expanding on these skills and following a predictable career trajectory. The typical career involved adopting a skill set, expanding upon it at the same company, and moving up the corporate ladder. This created a highly specialized workforce. Workers could not or would not readily move to another company. Not only would they lose their accrued benefits and the status they attained inside their firms, but they would also find it hard to find new work with a skill set so customized to a single company. Lastly, there was a negative assessment made of someone who (not out of necessity) job-hopped.

This command-and-control model reigned supreme for over thirty years, and during this time the company man reaped the benefits he was promised. The longest run of sustained growth in American history led to rising wages and an expansion of the middle class, which included blue-collar workers at the time. Growth and prosperity led to increased wages for so many Americans that the era has been termed the "Great Compression," so named for the decrease in economic inequality. The spread in the fortunes of Americans of different economic classes reached its lowest point ever.

However, by the late 1970s, workplace culture began to change in response to macroeconomic disruptions. American firms had become bloated affairs. This was no longer tenable in a new era of increased global competition. American manufacturing suffered as consumers began turning to imports over expensive American-made goods. The concurrent onset of the oil embargo and combined stagnant economy and inflation, "stagflation," in 1973 created a perfect storm that wrecked the American economy and erased many of the gains of the Great Compression. While the oil embargo ended in 1974, "stagflation" continued until 1982. Line workers in manufacturing were particularly at risk as they faced the threats of outsourcing, automation, and increased international competition. Unemployment rose. Wages fell. Keeping or finding a job and saving got harder for the American middle class, especially for those who worked in manufacturing.

This change was difficult for many, but definitely not for all. While the manufacturing sector saw one factory after another shuttered, service sectors actually expanded. Business consulting, financial services, health care, and the retail sector all grew. The knowledge economy was rising. The Oxford dictionary defines the knowledge economy as one in which growth is dependent on the quantity, quality, and accessibility of the information available, rather than the means of production. Services were in ascendence and manufacturing was in decline. Knowledge workers did very well in the new economy. Many even saw their prospects and compensation improve.

This new knowledge-based economy was very different than the one that came before. Jobs were changing. The nature of work was changing. Hiring practices were changing. Workers found that they could no longer rely on a specialized skill set that served only one company. The risks of being so overly specialized were significant. The economy and technologies were moving rapidly and becoming more fluid. Expanding on a single skill set in a predictable way was no longer a guaranteed ticket to a secure, sustainable middle-class life. Workers needed to become as adaptive as the labor markets had become. The covenant had been broken and companies no longer hired for life. Workers now needed to be willing to go where the jobs were.

Unsurprisingly, knowledge-based workers fared the best in the new economy. Those who could keep pace with technology and remain adaptive in the face of accelerating change were highly sought after and handsomely rewarded. These workers had portable skills that they could take with them from company to company. Those with in-demand skills could move from job to job without consequence. They were free agents, unlike the line workers and even white-collar company men with skill sets tailored to and honed at a specific company. Those workers did not fare well in the new economy unless they could retool and develop portable skill sets.

In his recent book *Range: Why Generalists Triumph in a Specialized World*, author David Epstein makes the case that generalists are better positioned for success than specialists in the modern economy, a claim that flies in the face of common knowledge about an economy that is increasingly specialized and advanced.

Epstein's argument makes sense when we consider how the new transactional workplace has changed incentives for workers and employers. While knowledge workers often have more expertise that we consider specialized, their skill sets are more portable because they have a broad application across the economy or at least across a thriving sector. Much of the training for these skill sets happens off the job, which is why it is so valuable to employers and is applicable across a whole industry or industries. Programmers, for example, can find work throughout the technology sector and also in the IT department of most large companies. Similarly, consultants can work for a variety of companies. These kinds of knowledge workers may fill highly specialized roles, but those roles can be found in a variety of companies and sectors.

Job-hopping and worker mobility worked to further unravel the covenant. In the new fast-paced economy, workers could no longer plan to grow with a company over the course of a lifetime. What the company wanted now might not be what it needed next year, much less next decade. Workers had to become more fluid and adaptable, which had the side effect of making them more mobile and interchangeable. The portable skill sets of knowledge workers were in higher demand making it easier for workers to abandon ship for a new company.

This all created a feedback loop in which workers became less attached to companies and companies became less invested in workers. With workers more able to hop around, the assumption that they would remain loyal declined. Eventually, many companies stopped investing in their employees' long-term growth. Private pensions and other long-term benefits disappeared, as they no longer made sense in an economy in which workers no longer stayed with companies for life.

Pension plans were originally offered by fast-growing firms in order to keep and attract talent during a tight labor market. Those pension plans were and are expensive to maintain. Funding them risked making firms less competitive because they were paid for out of corporate earnings, money that couldn't be invested back into the company. The elimination and/or reduction of this benefit, in turn, further dis-incentivized workers to stay loyal. It was no longer frowned upon to hop between jobs and companies. In the past, doing so was seen as flaky. Now, it is the norm, much to the chagrin of some boomers who still respect job tenure.

What We Gain and Lose with the Transactional Labor Market

The breaking of the covenant ended the era of the company man and ushered in the transactional labor market, a whole new model of employment. Gone was the lifelong commitment between employers and employees. In the new transactional model, workers perform X for employers and receive Y in return. There is no longer a sense of long-term commitment in these arrangements.

This is a big change. Under the old model, the company man was working for an implied future reward. He might have had a defined or deferred pension, but even this required the faith that the employer would honor the promise. In a transactional labor market, employment contracts and terms are defined, not implied. They have to be because the exchange is immediate. Both sides know exactly what they are entering into. They are bargaining for the here and now, not for the future.

The breaking of the covenant ensures that the transaction is a tit-for-tat exchange in the present. Deferred promises of compensation are meaningless when the employment contract is likely to be severed sooner rather than later. Workers want to know what is on offer for them right now. For their part, companies cannot expect blind, unconditional loyalty. Of course, many boomers still pine for loyalty from younger workers. "Whatever happened to loyalty to the organization?" they may wonder, bemoaning the lack of commitment from employees without also interrogating the company's lack of commitment *to* the employee.

There are still occasional pockets of the old "company man" model. Most companies recognize the cost of turnover and work hard to retain and keep staff. But, given the challenge in doing so, these companies are usually doing one of three things right. They are offering better compensation, attending to employees' wants and needs, or hiring in a location where other employment options are scarce. Otherwise, retaining staff over the long haul is difficult unless the firms have some form of options that are tied to performance and paid at some point in the future.

The transactional labor market's footprints can be observed across the entire economy. Consider the disappearance of private-sector pensions, which are virtually extinct. While some companies do still incentivize loyalty by offering employees benefits and retirement compensation that don't fully vest for a specified number of years, these arrangements are seldom for life. Typically, vesting periods are four to five years. Workers can no longer be enticed by the promise or implication of rewards any further out, as few stay with companies for life, so companies have nothing to gain from offering such incentives and conversely possibly much to lose if they do.

Perhaps the most extreme example of the transactional labor market is the "gig economy." This includes jobs at Uber, a self-employed taxi service; Fiverr, a freelance business services provider; and TaskRabbit, another freelance service provider that offers help with both work and home tasks. Gig workers are effectively freelancers. These gigs lack the stability of a job within an organization and may create a sense of looming anxiety due to their precarious nature. However, they may also be a good fit for some workers. They may complement Gen X sensibilities of independence or fulfill the millennial workers' search for purpose in work. These gigs may also appeal to the most entrepreneurial of generations, Gen Z. However, the precariousness of such a hyper-transactional labor market can be difficult on anyone.

Workers are having to adapt; flexibility and resilience are key. Workers must adjust to the new reality of the transactional labor market. Unfortunately, not everyone is fully embracing this model or thriving in it. This includes boomers, many of whom have found it hard to adjust to the new lay of the land. Their worldview was formed under the covenant. Many boomers are still dismayed by young people that show up for an interview and start asking about benefits and vacation time before a job offer is even extended. Boomers would never have dared to ask such questions when applying to entry-level jobs. They would have felt lucky for a job at a company that they could grow with over time.

This growth was the assumption. It didn't have to be stated—it was *implied*. Boomers trusted that, so long as they did the work and stayed the course, they would eventually be rewarded for their loyalty.

Today, the younger millennial, and their soon-to-be hired Gen Z brethren, believe that their time with a company is limited. They want to know what is on offer *now*. Employment contracts are a transaction between two parties, and they are one of those parties. Millennials and Gen Zers aren't just interested in showing what they can bring to the table—they also what to know what's in it for *them*.

As a boomer, had I been audacious enough to ask, "What's in it for me?" I would surely have landed on the street. No employer would have put up with that question forty years ago. But times have changed. The workers entering the workforce now see themselves entering a major financial transaction and want to understand the terms fully. We boomers are particularly shocked by this attitude of the millennials and Gen Zers because it wasn't displayed by Gen X, who entered the workforce during great market volatility and societal upheaval.

A question to consider: Is the transactional model better than the company man model?

The jury is still out, but it seems to be favoring those whom Daniel Markovits, author of *The Meritocracy Trap*, describes as the superordinate worker. These individuals are the meritocratic elite workers who make up a large portion of the 1 percent income earners that are capturing significant financial gains based on their much sought-after skills. The best we can say is that the transactional model is different and likely here to stay.

The transactional labor market does have clear benefits for many workers. For one, young workers can leverage their skills and talents for better jobs and pay. They can extract the full value of their labor and training instead of moving up the same lock-step trajectory that the company man followed. This is especially true for knowledge workers, whose portable skill sets make them competitive across a far wider and more diverse spectrum, for a variety of companies and roles.

Second, a transactional labor market is transparent and straightforward. Employment was *always* a transaction, just one in which the terms were often implied and many of the rewards were delayed. We now simply acknowledge the transactional nature of employment, especially in this new age. Say what you will about the transactional labor market, at least both parties know what to expect of each other. Companies and workers have little sense of long-term loyalty to each other in the new economy. The notion of loyalty between companies and their workers is no longer a norm but rather an exception—we do ourselves no favors complaining about either the employer's or the employee's commitment. The transactional labor market is merely a response to the new economy. Loyalty, when it exists today in direct personal relationships between employees and their managers or employer, is an outcome of promises kept, not promises made.

Despite the greater transparency and honesty in the exchange, both parties lose something in the shift toward the transactional model. More transparency hasn't resulted in greater trust between employers and workers. On the contrary, workers and employers now trust each other less than ever before. The short-term nature of the arrangement keeps workers and employers on guard. Workers understand that they are being hired for their skill set, not their loyalty, and are therefore highly replaceable. Employers know that workers might jump ship at any time, which has made them skeptical of their own employees.

Career mobility comes at a cost. Workers may never feel at home in their jobs. They're always thinking about the next move. Minor dissatisfactions or problems at work can get workers thinking about greener pastures whereas in the past, under the company man model, they would have learned to adapt and work through problems.

While workers can leave at any time, they don't necessarily do so. In *It's the Manager*, authors Jim Clifton and Jim Harter note that dissatisfied workers typically won't take a new job unless the total compensation package is significantly higher than what they are receiving from their current employer. According to *Business Insider*[12], anyone who is looking for a new job typically tries to negotiate an increase of between 10 to 20 percent higher than their present salary. Otherwise, jumping ship may not be worth the hassle. So, while switching jobs can be inconvenient, many knowledge workers *can* hop jobs at any time. Inertia, however, often keeps them from actually doing so. Knowing that they could leave, but that it isn't quite worth it, can actually make workers more dissatisfied than they would be if they didn't even have the option. Younger knowledge workers with desirable skill sets are thus both the most mobile workers in the new economy and also the most dissatisfied at work.

Of course, not all workers can be so mobile. Gen X workers and older millennials with children may accept greater dissatisfaction, at least temporarily, due to the negative repercussions a job change might have on their families. However, this is still different from boomers, who were more likely to pull up stakes and move if an

---

[12] Aine Cain, "How much money to ask for during your next salary negotiation," *Business Insider, July 18, 2018* https://www.businessinsider.com/how-much-money-to-ask-for-in-a-salary-negotiation-2015-5

employer asked it of them. This is why boomers are likely to interpret employees turning down transfers more negatively. Younger workers might see this as simply putting family first; whereas, boomers might interpret this as being uncommitted to the job.

Within the transactional labor market, workers do not only tend to doubt their employers, but they may also doubt *each other*. Workers understand that they are replaceable and therefore they are or can be in competition with each other. They may be kicked off a team and put out of a job if they cannot adapt to the role. This creates a level of pressure that yesteryear's company man didn't face. The company man was expected to adapt to any role, but he wasn't competing against a pool of other highly specialized workers from outside the company. Under the company man model, employers invested in individuals and valued their loyalty. They moved workers around and trusted that they would eventually adapt to new roles. The company man didn't fear being let go so much as simply not being promoted.

In the old days, bad employees that were loyal were often kept around. I'm old enough to remember how some of these people seemed to end up in Personnel Department. This department, which years later would be known as Human Resources (HR), was the elephant's graveyard for affable, well-liked, and well-connected workers with obsolete skill sets. (HR professionals need not take offense. This is not the case today, as HR professionals now have one of the most difficult jobs in industry . . . building and sustaining an engaged and committed workforce.)

Team cohesion also suffers under these conditions. There was a real sense of community under the company man model. Companies would hire teams of people who worked alongside each other year after year for decades. Coworkers got to know each other and became invested in each other. The transactional model has replaced these stable communities with a workplace in which the individual's agenda takes precedence over the needs of the team. This is reinforced by the fact that we don't necessarily reward teams—we reward individuals on teams. Couple this emphasis on the individual with coworkers who are "here today, may be gone tomorrow" and the ties that bind teams together are loosened or even eliminated.

This could really be a problem as Gen X continues to take more and more leadership positions. Being so self-sufficient, they may not see team cohesion as an issue. Millennials, whose upbringing has made them more collaborative by nature, are likely to find atomized and disconnected teams far more upsetting. (More on this later.)

The collapse of private-sector unions only accelerated the collapse of worker solidarity, community, and trust. Today, most workers negotiate as individuals, not as collectives. According to the Bureau of Labor Statistics union membership peaked in 1954, when almost 35 percent of all employed American workers were union members, but this number had fallen to just 10 percent in 2020.

While workers can leverage their skill sets for maximum compensation on an open market, they are no longer able to bargain collectively. They are in competition with one another. The more unique your skill set, the more leverage you have in the marketplace, but few workers qualify as the superordinate elite and fewer still are truly irreplaceable. The drawback of portable skill sets is that, while you can hop to a new job, someone else can also easily fill yours.

The transactional nature of the labor market has commoditized even knowledge workers. They are free to move from job to job, yes—but, for doing so, companies have come to see workers as interchangeable. They are hiring the skill set, not the person.

This creates a high-pressure job market in which young workers must always be improving their skill set to remain competitive. Remaining competitive in such a fluid labor market isn't easy. Paradoxically, the work-life balance and career flexibility that many millennials have been seeking have created an environment in which they are working more and harder than ever.

Much of this self-improvement must be done "off the clock." This is not just because knowledge jobs often require training and education, though they do. For some companies, it feels counterintuitive to train or develop their own employees since they may just pick up and leave in a year or two. In fact, the transactional labor market creates disincentives to develop employees. Training workers increases their portability and value in the labor market, making it more likely that they will get a better offer and leave. (I am reminded of a Henry Ford quote: "The only thing worse than training your employees and having them leave, is not training them, and having them stay.")

This is very different from the company man model, which, for all of its faults, incentivized companies to invest in employees. The company man grew with the company, moving up in lockstep with others at the same level. Companies were more willing to train and develop employees when the company's needs were more stable and the workers were less mobile. They weren't hiring the skill set so much as the person that they could depend on for the duration—and there was no more valuable personal trait than loyalty. The reward for loyalty was advancement. They had to perform well, of course, but companies willing to invest in workers didn't hire based on skills they could train. They hired and promoted based on potential and loyalty. The employees in this bygone era were less mobile in the job market, but they were also more secure at the company. They were not easily replaceable; the work and their positions were not easily commoditized not so much by the job description alone but by the way they worked in a culture unique to the organization. However, a secure position can also be a stifling one.

Gen Z is even more aligned with the transactional labor market. As a generational cohort, they place a high value on equity and fairness, even more so than the millennials. The most diverse generation to have ever existed, Gen Z demands equal treatment regardless of class, race, gender, or other identities. This isn't about equality of outcomes—it's about transparency and fair transactions. They want equal pay for equal work. Echoing the traits of independence and individualism that their Gen X (and first-wave millennial) parents exhibited, Gen Z is shaping up to be somewhat less collaborative than millennials. They will be quite unhappy pulling weight for coworkers that get paid the same for doing less. Armed with modern tracking technology, they will have access to metrics that prove how much they are working. Taken all together, this may only serve to ratchet up the tit-for-tat transactional model.

Where Do We Go from Here?

There is no rolling back the clock on the transactional labor market and the post-covenant economy. It is here to stay—and that isn't necessarily a bad thing. The fact is that many millennials like transparent transactional working arrangements. Young knowledge workers have benefited from the ability to leverage their skill sets for better pay. Most millennials, on a voyage toward self-discovery in life and at work, would abhor the notion of being locked into the same company for life unless, of course, the company evolves and changes as they do. They have embraced being able to move around and try different things, as it is a way for them to explore and realize different versions of themselves.

The transactional labor market is the new reality, and struggling against that reality will likely prove futile. What companies and managers *can* do is embrace the benefits of transactional labor while working to ameliorate many of its harms. Managers must instead work within the paradigm, which means working *with*, not against, their own workers. The transactional labor market has many pros that workers are not willing to give up. We should embrace these benefits and not look down on young workers for trying to negotiate at the bargaining table. We should not get angry with workers that leave after a few years—that's simply the name of the game. These young people are advocating for themselves in a working environment that requires it of them. They cannot depend on the company to take care of them, so they simply take care of themselves. The future as I see it will be "lopsided" (more on that shortly). We will embrace that which is unique to the people in our employ. The teams they will be a part of will work collaboratively and leverage teammates' unique perspectives and strengths in service of collective gains meanwhile distributing rewards for not just individuals but for their teams as well.

Rather than berating young workers for hopping jobs, we should instead be working to provide what they are looking for. If they seek growth and challenge or variety, that can—to some degree—be provided in the same company. Workers can and will leave and move around, but they will do so less often when their existing employers provide a better deal. This isn't just about money. It is also about the nature of work and how it fits into worker's lives.

It is certainly true that companies have to be prudent in how they invest in developing workers in the new economy. If we can accept that both workers and employers have something to gain from a well-trained workforce, then we should all be able to agree that these investments can and should be made in a collaborative, supportive, win-win manner. Both parties getting at least some of what they want serves as a foundation for trust that ultimately leads to greater productivity and that elusive trait, loyalty.

Furthermore, those millennials that do leave in search of new challenges or the Gen Xers that moved for higher pay may discover that the grass wasn't greener after all . . . and some may well come boomeranging back. If they are good performers, we should set aside our sensibilities about what constitutes being "disloyal" and welcome them back into the fold.

Part Two

Changes at Work

Chapter 7: The Balance Myth

"You have to balance your passions, not your time."

Lisa Sugar

Thousands of self-help gurus have penned millions of words on how to achieve "work-life balance." It is generally a euphemism for the dissatisfaction people feel from spending an inordinate amount of time on the *non-productive* aspects of work instead of the care and feeding of their lives outside of work. The operative phrase here is the *non-productive* aspects of work; I will argue that if work consisted of doing those things that we truly enjoyed then we most likely wouldn't use the term work to describe those things, nor would we be in any way concerned about having balance. Perhaps no book better encapsulates this ethos than Timothy Ferriss's wildly popular *The 4-Hour Work-week*, which promises to help readers leverage passive income streams to achieve financial independence while having more free time. This is not a novel concept. The same advice can be found in the book's many predecessors and gets repeated *ad nauseam* by copycats. Blogs and online forums dedicated to "FI/RE," an acronym for financial independence and retire early, allow people to share similar tips and tricks for escaping the daily grind.

Well before self-help authors were peddlling shortcuts to this utopic vision of the good life, economists and technologists had long promised that humankind will someday soon be freed from the daily grind—or, at the very least, be able to contain it to a few hours a day. Keep in mind dear reader, this utopian vision was a reaction to Fredrick W. Taylor, the father of the scientific management approach to work. Among his few key principles, Taylor suggested breaking work down into its component parts and subsequently reorganize those parts to maximize efficiency. Efficiency gains were supposed to allow people to finish their work in a fraction of the time, but efficiency gains came at a cost. This maximizing of efficiency resulted in ceding control over one's work to others. The work itself became, at best, simply repetitious. And now, tasks broken down to simply their constituent parts have become vulnerable to automation as those jobs avail themselves to be done by computers, machines, and robots.

So far, these predictions have proved little more than wishful thinking, at least in terms of shortening the workday. Technology *has* increased efficiency and automated countless jobs away, but, somehow, we always seem to find new things for people to do. In his 2018 book *Bullshit Jobs*, author David Graeber argues that more than half of the work now performed in the United States provides no real value. Even when workers are being productive, their increased efficiency actually means that they are put to work more. The Jevons paradox, as articulated by the nineteenth-century economist William Stanley Jevons, shows that efficient consumption of resources leads to more consumption, not less. Burn coal more efficiently and it does more work, increasing the utility and therefore exploitation of coal. The same rules apply to human resources. The more work you do per hour, the more profitable it is for the boss to have you on the clock.

The ever-promised end of work is *not* on the horizon, not for the foreseeable future. And it is not the work itself that I hold in disrepute, it is those aspects of work we deem meaningless to the true contributions we make to the organization. This issue is not being able to control how we do what we do and why we do it. It should come as no surprise, that many of us are fixated on the idea of working less so that we might enjoy life more. There is a sad irony when individuals, through hard work and personal sacrifice, achieve material success in life at the expense of having a life outside of their work.

Americans pride themselves on their work ethic while secretly longing for meaning in life that the work doesn't seem to provide. We work feverishly to build a nest egg for retirement. Retiring at sixty-five to enjoy your golden years is becoming more and more elusive. The new American dream, for some, is to retire early, in your thirties or forties if possible. While the numbers show that few can actually retire early, the inordinate amount of ink spilled on the subject indicates that many hope to do so. In the meantime, many of us want more time to escape from the pressure of work and in so doing spend more time with family, pursue leisure, or explore the best Netflix has to offer.

This is how work-life balance is depicted in the popular consciousness, but it needn't be this way.

Lifestyle Creep versus Work-Life Balance—Why So Many Are So Unhappy

You may have heard the saying, "Life is what happens outside of work," and there is a hidden assumption in this line of thinking. The concept of work-life balance takes as given that work is separate from the rest of life. This notion, under which most of us boomers were raised, held true for us in our early years in the workplace. As children, when Dad came home, he didn't work over or through dinner. He ate. He watched TV. He tinkered about the house. As working adults, boomers took the cue. They showed up to the office early, worked all day, and left late. It was only a few hours afterward, if there were any at all, that the boomers considered "free time." In order to separate work and life, work was cordoned off as its own discrete thing. From this perspective, work is strictly work, something to be done at the workplace so that we can get on with the fun and exciting stuff that makes up our "actual" lives. Our time off work is when we pursue leisure, hobbies, relationships, and our "real" interests.

As I mentioned at the beginning of this chapter, not all work is seen or felt as working. If you are engaged in activities you find fulfilling, that allow you a sense of control, that give you purpose, and that draw on your strengths then we don't think in terms of spending "less" time at work. We may not even consider it work. But if your work is a series of tasks and time that is not your own, then the desire to escape from it will lead one to seek a greater work-life balance. Work in its most clinical sense is what we do for others, not ourselves, and not because we necessarily want to but because we have been hired to do so. When others ask of us that which requires only compliance that is *their* time—*our* time is everything else. Conversely, if the work is presented in such a way that we willingly commit to it then we move from simply working to engaging. We have a fulfilling purpose. Sadly, when that which we spend most of our waking hours doing doesn't provide us with meaning, many of us separate work from literally everything else in life. The result for many working Americans is that there is life and then there is work. Generally, we yearn for more of the former and less of the latter.

The truth is that in the context of business, work-life balance is a relatively recent notion, unique to rich, highly developed societies with the privilege of being able to treat modern comforts as needs. On a societal level, working mothers have been dealing with this since they first entered the workforce, balancing the needs of their families with the needs of their employers. According to Nancy R. Lockwood, a Human Resources content expert, she stated in her research paper, *Work/Life Balance Challenges and Solutions*, the term work-life balance came into popular use in 1986.[13] I am being speculative, but I believe it was second-wave boomers and first-wave Gen X women who likely voiced it. They were present in the workplace in sufficient numbers to be heard and, if they were part of a household, were more likely to have more responsibilities in maintaining it while working full time outside the home. Improving work-life balance was sought to remedy this imbalance.

In the United States, and many other developed nations, middle-class citizens are able to meet their basic needs without substantial existential struggle. Yes, we all struggle, but not for

---

[13]   Nancy R. Lockwood, "Work/Life Balance Challenge and Solutions", *SHRM Research Quarterly*, 2003, 2nd qtr. http://adapt.it/adapt-indice-a-z/wp-content/uploads/2014/06/lockwood_work_life_balance_2003.pdf

our very lives, not as a matter of routine. The middle class has no trouble meeting its true needs, by which I mean food, shelter, safety, and the other necessities down at the base of Maslow's hierarchy of needs.

It is only as we approach the top the pyramid that we start lumping modern luxuries into the needs pile. Many of our "needs" are luxury goods and modern conveniences that didn't even exist earlier in our lifetimes. Personal computers, hi-definition televisions, smartphones, high-speed internet, cars for every member of the family over sixteen, and large detached single-family housing are now needs for the average middle-class family.

Some of these are arguably real needs in many American communities. Try getting to work without a car in most of suburban America—you won't get far. But it is harder to claim that a car for every member of the nuclear family is really a need. It is hard to consider a new car or a luxury car a "need." But many do. Give someone enough money and a simple phone won't do—it must be the latest smartphone. Homes have to be constantly updated and regularly remodeled with the latest features and all the fixings. An NPR report[14] from 2006 cited that in 1950, the average size of a home was 950 square feet (while the average household had 3.37 members). According to the U.S. Census Bureau, the average new home built in 2015 was 2,687 square feet (while the average household size dropped to 3.14).

In defense of humanity, we are hard wired to seek out new experiences. Daniel Gable, in his book, *Alive at Work: The Neuroscience of Helping Your People Love What They Do*, writes humans

---

14 Margot Adler, "Behind the Ever-Expanding American Dream House," *NPR*, July 4, 2006 https://www.npr.org/templates/story/story.php?storyId=5525283

beings are "seeking systems." We are born to be curious, and we find excitement in exploring and making new discoveries. What is missing in many of our working lives is the opportunity to employ our "seeking systems" at work. Instead, we may compensate after work and seek material substitutes.

This substitution is compounded by social pressure to broadcast our own success. In modern society, with the pressures of survival removed, we have the time to be constantly comparing our situation to the circumstances of our neighbors and peers. Sometimes our need for a new television is less about the thing itself and more about what it signals. Posting that pic of the shiny new car fresh off the dealership lot is a modern "need" of its own. This has never been truer than in the present, when so much of our lives is shared for all on social media.

My intent here is not to shame, judge, or condemn. I am a classic "seeking system" when it comes to cars and art. While I am of a generation that is more skeptical and wary of social media than the young, I am as guilty as the next boomer of trying to "keep up with the Joneses." I am also guilty of lifestyle creep. If I were to move from my comfortable neighborhood on Chicago's near northside I would likely look for a place that is at least equivalent to my existing neighborhood. Otherwise, I might mourn the loss of not only my home but the unspoken status that the neighborhood affords me.

This is all just human nature. Daniel Gable noted that humans are by their nature driven by our interests and curiosity. We are yearning for the next acquisition or achievement. We are naturally inclined to show off to our peers. In a developed and growing economy, it only makes sense that our wants and "needs" are always expanding.

If in our pursuit of work-life balance the work lacks meaning, purpose, and engagement, then it is incompatible with never-ending lifestyle creep—and it can and will make us miserable if we are not careful. We may *say* we want more leisure time, but our actions belie the claim. We continue to strive harder and harder, working more and more, which makes us susceptible to messages claiming to unlock the secret to earning more while doing less.

Work Now, Live Later: the Siren Song of Deferred Reward

Lifestyle creep is not the only thing incompatible with the pursuit of work-life balance. The shift from the "company man" corporate model to the transactional labor market, as discussed in the previous chapter, is also making people less satisfied with how work fits into their modern lives.

Following World War II, many soldiers came home to a "revitalized" United States. The war engine went back to manufacturing consumer goods, rather than military equipment, but with much greater capacity. The New Deal programs ushered in an era of unmatched economic expansion and equality. These were good years for the American middle class. Many veterans took well-paying factory jobs that allowed them to raise families in blue-collar jobs similar to their white-collar counterparts. They received G.I. loans to pursue higher education or buy homes. It is hard to overstate the mental shift that occurred in the populace.

For decades, a whole generation had learned to ration and make do. The depression and the war effort had hardened people and taught them to do without. Those hard times were now at an end. The lean years of the Great Depression and the rationing of all goods and supplies during World War II had finally passed. Americans were finally able to indulge—and the party was just starting. For the next thirty years, the United States enjoyed economic expansion, a stretch of rapid, sustained economic growth that was unprecedented and hasn't been seen since.

This period was named the Great Compression, for the fact that economic expansion coupled with social welfare initiatives and strong, healthy unions flattened wage differentials. There were still poor people, though fewer of them, and the rich were still the rich. But the middle class was growing and thriving like never before (and never since). It was a good time to be an *average* American. A man (yes, generally only a man) could pay a mortgage and support a family on a single median income while his wife raised the kids and managed the home. The employer-employee covenant was still in good standing, and the American employee was confident that his employer would take care of him for life.

The covenant would eventually be broken. The working world now is so different that it can be hard to convey what it was like before. We have seen a number of economic expansions in the decades since then, but they have not had the same character as the Great Compression. The Great Compression wasn't *just* a time of unfettered economic growth for most companies. The model for that growth was wholly different from what we have now. Companies and labor markets operated in a fundamentally different way than they do now. The economy of the Great Compression operated under different rules that were inherited from the wartime economy. Competition was domestic, not global, economic growth was assured year after year, labor had a strong voice in how companies operated, and pensions provided security in retirement.

The transition from the command-and-control wartime economy to a civilian one produced a very specific work ethic and business culture. The work could be very hard. It wasn't called the military-industrial complex for grins. This was serious business. You weren't just working for your employer—you were working for the good of the country and the free world. When you were on the clock, you worked hard. However, when the whistle blew, you were off, and it was time to play. You left work behind at the factory. There was no email to answer from home, no texts, no Zoom calls, or after-hour conference calls. After the assembly line had been shut down for the day, you went home.

This work culture fed into a larger American culture that treated work and life as binaries rather than work as a subset of life. At the time, many workers were actually quite happy with this arrangement. They were not yet bringing work home with them, as we do today. While they were working hard, their work stayed at work. Rank-and-file workers were rarely expected to be available around the clock, 24-7. Their time off was their own in a way that isn't nearly as true today. While the work-life dichotomy remains part of the American consciousness, work now bleeds into the home, which has left many contemporary workers frustrated.

This is not the only way in which our modern working condition is very different from life under the covenant. The company man was working under the belief that the company would care for him for life. (Again, I used the words *he* and *him* here intentionally, as women largely exited the workforce to make room for the soldiers coming home from the war. Female employment was much lower at the time. In 1950, only one in three women participated in the labor force.)

The command-and-control structure and loyalty to his

employer were acceptable to the company man because he didn't have to worry about retirement. He wasn't just working for his nights and weekends—he was also working for his golden years. This could assuage any regrets he might have had about not being able to try new jobs at different companies. After all, he was free to pursue other interests on his own time or after he retired. The company man was working for a hypothetical deferred future reward when he could pursue his own life, both in the day-to-day/week-to-week and also on the macro level.

Deferring rewards in this way precluded the modern concept of work-life balance as we know it. Workers saw work as a discreet part of life, one that for some was less than pleasant but necessary, but they knew to keep their mouths shut. Sacrifice now and receive your rewards later. And those rewards were substantial—a pension, healthcare, and other retirement benefits. This kept the company man from complaining about his situation. Who in their right mind would have asked for more free time or "balance" in their lives with so much on the line? If someone was malcontent, brave, and misguided enough to make such a demand, his manager would have given him a look of befuddlement. The answer would almost certainly have been no, or, worse, "Sure, take all the free time you want. You're fired." And in a single moment, the company man loses everything that he has worked for up until that point. Who would dare risk it?

Furthermore, everyone was generally accepting of the company man model. As a carryover from the command-and-control wartime economy, the focus was on increasing production. Workers were seeing rewards for their contributions and loyalty with the promise of even greater reward in the future. As long as promises were kept, the model made a great deal of sense for everyone involved. After all, the same model had won the

United States the greatest war of all wars and it was now, during the Great Compression, providing a good life for a good many workers and families as they ascended into the middle class. It would have made no sense for these workers to demand more balance in their lives—never before in the country, or the world, had any generation of people had it so good.

Of course, the model ultimately collapsed when the employer-employee arrangement came to an end. The traditionalists and the very earliest of the baby boomers skated by on company-funded retirements, but many of the baby boomers saw the covenant broken only after they had put in decades of work on the promise of deferred compensation.

By the mid-1970s, the country was plagued with stagflation and the crippling effects of the oil embargo. The competition got stiffer, and companies began downsizing and "rightsizing," which meant letting go of workers before upholding their end of the bargain. Pensions were cut or renegotiated after the fact. People were let go. Workplaces closed. This wasn't limited to factories and workers on the assembly line. Managerial and white-collar jobs were on the chopping block as well. Domestic companies were competing with foreign producers offering goods at lower prices, and to remain competitive they had to restructure and cut costs to stay viable. Firms had to adapt to the new reality.

During this period, the corporate promise of lifetime employment still existed, for some, but the substantial cuts showed that the covenant was showing cracks. Its implicit agreements and promises of deferred compensation were not to be trusted.

The unraveling of corporate America's commitment to its employees set the conditions for changing attitudes for both employers and employees. Workers no longer had a promise of deferred compensation that kept them loyal until retirement.

This was a dream delayed. The economy was in a tailspin, shaken by macroeconomic changes and the oil shocks. The unemployment rate was flirting with double digits. After three decades of economic expansion, good jobs were suddenly hard to come by. Employers often had to take draconian measures to stay in business. Asking for more balance in one's life wasn't prudent when the employment landscape was very much a buyer's market. One needs a job to balance work against life. One needs a job to live a life at all, much less a life in balance.

Gen X: the Heralds of Work-Life Balance

The national obsession with work-life balance only really took off when Gen X entered and reformulated the workplace. *The Economist* astutely noted[15] that young Gen X technologists were the first generation to ever teach upward. Historically, most knowledge and know-how were passed down from the older generations to the new. Consider professions such as law: while law graduates may call themselves lawyers, they really need to work under experienced attorneys to become competent practitioners of the law. This squared well with the hierarchical command-and-control economy, especially for the many jobs in which workers honed a company-specific skill set. Institutional knowledge must be handed down from those within the institution. Workers learn their company-specific roles best from someone who has already been doing the work, managing the work, and ultimately overseeing the work.

---

15 "The Geek as Boss", *The Economist*, January 13, 2001 https://www.economist.com/business/2001/01/11/the-geek-as-boss

As children, Gen Xers witnessed the downsizing and euphemistic "right-sizing" that their parents endured. They took the lesson to heart and, as adults, knew that they couldn't rely on a single company to take care of them. In fact, realizing the value of their skills, the most entrepreneurial of these Gen X knowledge workers realized that they didn't need to depend on someone else's company at all. Rather than selling their skills to legacy companies, they used their expertise to establish their own companies, which gave birth to the dot-com boom.

The companies that these young knowledge workers founded often looked very different than the legacy companies that they had eschewed. These young Gen X entrepreneurs, driven by the self-sufficiency that they had picked up as a generation of latch-key kids, chose to do things their own way. Many reimagined the shape and nature of work. The dot-com workplaces were typically less formal, more egalitarian, and experimental in nature. This was basically the last nail in the coffin for the command-and-control economy, as clever young people worked out new ways to leverage technology to reimagine how work—and the workplace—should look. Demands for more work-life balance that workers had not been able to make at legacy companies in the command-and-control economy were first implemented by Gen X entrepreneurs. The experiment continues today as companies increasingly embrace flexibility and adaptability in the workplace. The pandemic will reverberate for years to come as it has accelerated this process of embracing flexible work schedules.

The most obvious manifestation of this flexibility is the rise of telecommuting and working from home. The proliferation of affordable home computers allowed the office to move into the home. By this time, many more women had entered the workplace, which meant that parents had less time with their families.

Many chose to work from home, and technology and creative companies priding themselves on flexibility and experimentation were often happy to let them. Again, the pandemic has made "Zoom meetings" not the exception but the rule for how a team might gather. This is only the tip of the iceberg as to how work processes will be changing in the coming years.

While these changes may sound positive, they were not without drawbacks. Working from home can be convenient. The flexibility can give workers more control over their own lives. However, this kind of work arrangement erodes the separation of work from the rest of life that was a hallmark of the command-and-control production economy. Workers were no longer able to leave work at work, especially not when the workplace was literally located in the home. Without an exceptional ability to compartmentalize, most people cannot wall work off from the rest of life when your office is literally in your home.

Work wasn't just bleeding into the home for telecommuters either. It was becoming the norm for all workers. In the modern economy, many professionals are expected to be available around the clock. People handle email and other work communication in the mornings and evenings, also over the weekend. We are now always *on*. It is no wonder that we crave more work-life balance when we participate in a technology-enabled, always-on environment.

Millennials and now Gen Z entered the workforce under this new paradigm. While boomers and Gen X had to learn to adapt, this is the only work world the younger generations have ever known. Because many are relatively new to the workplace and have not acquired entrenched habits, they see the good in it more than anything else. They also see flexibility, not as a benefit but rather a requirement, all to the ongoing consternation of the remaining boomers in the workplace.

Boomer Habits Die Hard

These changes were hardest on workers that did not grow up with them. While Gen X entrepreneurs set out to redefine the workplace, changing cultures within a workplace is not easy. Most employees, being human, are creatures of habit. Workplace cultures cannot be set or determined entirely from the top. They are the result of how workers interact within a set of conditions over time. While leadership can change the conditions, they cannot change the workers, not overnight. Culture is a sticky thing.

Let's step back for a moment and discuss culture in its broadest sense and then look at what that means for the culture within a company. Developing a model for understanding cross-cultural communication, linguist Richard D. Lewis, author of *When Cultures Collide*, identified three categories of cultural communication style: *linear active*, *multi-active*, and *reactive*.[16] No culture falls neatly into a single category. The categories exist on a triangular spectrum. Different countries and cultures fall somewhere in between, typically closer to one or two points on the triangle.

1. Linear active communication is singular, focused, planned, and scheduled. These kinds of cultures view time as a precious commodity. They are likely to believe that time is money. The Swiss and Germans fall more in this category.

2. Multi-active communication isn't so militant about time. It is more focused on building relationships when communicating. People with this cultural communication style are more likely to finish the conversation than adhere to a schedule. "No time

16 Richard D. Lewis, *When Cultures Collide: Leading Across Cultures* (Boston Nicolas Brealey International revised third edition: 2006).

like the present," they are apt to say. This communication style is associated with Spain and Italy.

3. Reactive cultures are those that value deference and courtesy in communication. People within these cultures will listen quietly and respectfully before reacting. Asian countries, such as Japan or China, exemplify this communication style.

These communication styles are reflections of different cultural norms. Given these differences, it is easy to understand why the trains in Switzerland run on time while those in Madrid often do not. Business meetings in Germany are generally scheduled, timely, and formal while those in Italy often start late, run long, and readily change directions. In this way, we can see cultural differences play out at the granular level in how people behave in business and elsewhere.

These are, of course, broad generalizations, and there are many forces and conditions that shape culture. My point is that culture develops over time and becomes normative for the group. These cultural habits are not easily washed away, especially not from the top-down. While Madrid might benefit from trains that run on time, the local culture doesn't emphasize timeliness. No one *expects* the trains to run on time, and so inertia has carried the day. The government hasn't moved to overhaul the transit system: they feel no pressure to fix that which they don't perceive to be broken.

This same effect can be observed in other areas of Spanish culture. While many firms strive to observe global norms for business, if you have ever traveled to or lived in Spain, as I was privileged to have done, you know that many Spaniards still take mid-morning coffee breaks and may leave midday for a late lunch and "siesta" before returning to the office. The pace of work seems less hectic, but this rhythm appears to suit their culture and their people. It is what they have always known.

As the world, particularly the corporate world, continues to globalize, Spanish culture has had to evolve and better conform to global business practices. This has been a sea change for the Spanish, and possibly a loss of cultural richness for the rest of the world. While living in Spain, the Spanish way of life struck me as romantic. I could never have lived that way myself. As an American, having grown up in a linear-active society, I would have felt strange leaving work in the middle of the day only to come back again that afternoon. Why would I want to commute twice?

Ironically, I wasn't working in Spain during this time. My visa didn't permit it. My days were spent sightseeing, reading, and trying to learn the language. I went out at night to immerse myself in the language and the people. This was all terribly exciting and fun . . . at first. Eventually, guilt set in. I felt lazy and unaccomplished while not working. My American linear-active cultural habits were spoiling my fun. Upon returning home to the States, I got a job and went to work like everyone else around me. Though the guilt dissipated, I sometimes missed the freedom of having my days entirely to myself. However, as an American boomer and the product of a Protestant work ethic, it never occurred to me to redesign my life to include more flexibility. What was I thinking?

This was the result of my upbringing. As an American baby boomer, I believed that it was important to get a good education so that you could get a good job. Work was the number one priority in life, and it always came before play. People who didn't stay late at the office and put in extra work weren't "serious" people. Work came first except during your two weeks of vacation every year, maybe three or four if you stuck it out a few decades. The rest of the year, work came first before all else.

Clearly, we boomers had no sense of work-life balance. I had never even heard of the concept until Gen X started reshaping the modern workplace. Despite bearing witness to the changes in workplace culture and spending much of my own life studying its changes over the generations, I don't think about "balance" in my work-life.

As an independent practitioner, I do not have a formal boss, but even if I did, I could not imagine petitioning them for more balance. I still think of work as the first priority and balance as something to figure out in my free time. Unfortunately, boomers in the workplace may be prone to reacting negatively to younger workers asking for more work-life balance. One reason is how we interpret the request. If you are someone who is prioritizing work and life, then work comes before free time in your priorities. It would follow you would perceive the person making the request as putting their personal lives before work. What we may fail to understand is that it may not be about the relative importance of work but rather for flexibility in how the work is done. Even more importantly, it is a request to make the work itself more engaging.

While many of us boomers adapted to the demands for work-life balance that arose from the transactional labor market, we never really warmed to the concept. Interestingly, those boomers who have embraced work-life balance often did so not for their own sake but for that of others. Young boomers did not dare to advocate for themselves—that would have suggested that they were not serious people wholly committed to their work. Instead, many boomers now in leadership championed the concept of balance as a way to attract talent among the new generation of workers. These workers were more likely to give weight to personal interests as well as professional ones. If we would take the time to explore what was behind the request, we might find common ground.

Younger boomers and older Gen X managers can find themselves "sandwiched" caretaking for both children and aging parents. But, sadly, most of us boomers are still unable to find balance for ourselves. The pandemic has allowed us to reexamine our existing attitudes and habits toward work and experiment with new ways of working. We need not lecture them for not having our work ethics if we can accept there are multiple ways of getting the work done. What we need to do is find ways to make the work itself more engaging.

From Balancing to Integrating

The concept of work-life balance has morphed and evolved over the approximately forty years it has been with us. Each generational wave has ushered in a new take on how work best fits into life. In a sense, work-life balance is something of a misnomer, as every generation has had a different take on the relationship between work and the rest of life. Lumping them all into the same moniker, which fits no version of the concept perfectly, is misleading.

Boomers working under the command-and-control economy that were able to "leave work at work" were probably the living generation that came closest to actually achieving work-life balance. Many of them actually did have discreet professional lives that were separate from their personal lives, although the mix was always skewed toward work. We worked at work and we played at home, and never the twain shall meet (until, of course, they did).

Gen X was never truly balancing work with life. They may not exhibit the same approach to work as the boomers, but they are pragmatic and realists. They understand that work eclipses all else in our business-first world. There is no balancing work with life, not in a world where we spend most of our waking hours at work only to bring that work home with us too. As the experiments that Gen X undertook in building a more flexible workplace were really aimed at accommodating work in a greater life, a better term for the Gen X mindset might be *work-life accommodation*.

Gen X recognized the difficulty in truly balancing work with a personal life while still expecting to succeed professionally. Work still had to come first. The best they could hope to do was build a workplace that allowed enough flexibility to allow for shifting priorities and needs in one's personal life. Flexible work arrangements allowed them to fit their professional lives around their personal lives. They could shift work hours in order to drive the kids to and from school. Unfortunately, in the United States, only some parents are afforded a reasonable amount of maternity (and now paternity) leave. These accommodations sometimes helped them navigate work that was taking up more and more of their time, but it was certainly not a rebalancing of the importance of work. Work maintained its primacy—it simply became easier to accommodate into one's life.

This is very different from the millennial mindset, which can be described as *work-life integration*. This too should not be mistaken for balance. Millennials are not doing a better job of balancing their personal lives with work than Gen X has been. Instead, they have worked to integrate work into their personal lives. They are breaking down the walls between their professional and personal lives. Compared to previous generations, fewer millennials are clocking into nine-to-five jobs. Many are cobbling together careers in the gig economy and pursuing part-time or flexible work arrangements. This is sometimes out of necessity. The Great Recession and then the COVID-19 global pandemic have made it hard for some young people to find full-time jobs, but for others, it is an elective lifestyle choice.

Millennials are sometimes referred to as "slashers." They are not just a programmer but a programmer/photographer. They are not just a customer service rep but a customer service rep/artist. Millennials are taking on multiple roles to explore different experiences in pursuit of finding themselves. The slasher phenomenon is not restricted to those with part-time jobs or driving for Uber on the weekend. Many millennials with full-time jobs still identify as slashers. A millennial working in a law office by day and pursuing an interest in fine wine at night might be a paralegal/sommelier. A millennial nurse might work three shifts at the hospital and spend the other days working on an event planning business.

We must understand the slasher trend as more than just economic survival, especially now that it continues well beyond the Great Recession and into a post-pandemic world. This is a search for meaning. Millennials, sometimes called "generation me," have always valued self-exploration and self-reflection. Their parents raised them to be exploratory and self-reflective—it worked. They treat their work lives as expressions of their true self and see jobs as a part of self-discovery on the path to see who they will become in life. In this way, they have always tried to integrate work into their lives in a way that feels authentic and true to who they are. They are not balancing work against life—they are integrating the two as fully as possible.

Lucky for them, millennials are a generation adept at integration. We can see this in their relationship to modern technology.

While technology made Gen X the first generation able to teach up, most of them were already adults by the time personal computers became ubiquitous in the home. They were getting established in their careers by the time internet, smartphones, or social media became staples of modern life. This was not the case for millennials, especially the latter half of the generation, who grew up alongside these technologies. Millennials entering the workplace were often using technology at home that surpassed what was being used in the workplace. Many millennials brought in tech from home in order to integrate technology from their personal lives into their professional lives.

Eventually, many companies relented somewhat on these policies and adapted to millennials. They had no choice—millennial knowledge workers have even more portable skill sets than their Gen X predecessors. They have more leverage in the transactional labor market than any previous generation. They are, in a sense, transactional "natives" whereas those who came before were transactional "immigrants" who had to adapt to the new transactional labor market. Companies wanting to attract top millennial talent have to accept the ways in which millennials are integrating work into their lives.

Often, what millennials strive for are more flexible work arrangements that allow them to pursue multiple interests simultaneously. Given that telecommuting is now so accessible, firms wanting to keep millennials in the office have had to take extreme measures to do so. Cutting-edge companies in "sexy" sectors, such as tech, offer perks to keep workers in the office. Silicon Valley companies offer on-site entertainment and concierge services. Break rooms are stocked with the latest game consoles. Personal trainers, meditation rooms, and yoga instructors are viable options. Technology workers are being offered a "gilded cage" just to keep them at work. These practices have become so prevalent in the tech industry that even many legacy companies are following suit in order to compete for top talent.

Why would anyone work in the IT department of a fusty old bank when Facebook is offering onsite masseuses and yoga at work? The world is a different place. This is the problem that companies face in retaining top talent. They aren't just trying to keep millennials in the office—they are struggling to keep them in the *company*. The labor market is more transactional than ever and workers with in-demand skill sets can jump from one company to the next in pursuit of a better quality of life. Gen Zers, who are now entering the workforce in large numbers don't see flexible work schedules as a benefit but rather as a require-ment. Saying to a Gen Zer at a job interview that you offer flexible working arrangements is like saying to them they'll get to work in a building with doors. Gosh, no kidding, real doors?

While the Gen Z identity is still developing, they seem to be continuing on many of the trends observed with millennials. Gen Z appears to be even more entrepreneurial than millennials. Like the millennials, they never knew the covenant unbroken and have never expected employers to take care of them. However, they also understand that societal safety nets are in a precarious state. Not only can Gen Z not expect a pension, which is now a nostalgic notion, they can't even be certain that Medicare and Social Security will be there when they retire. Couple this knowl-edge with the fact that Gen Z watched millennials and their own parents struggle during the Great Recession, and it is easy to see why they are more fiscally conservative. I do not mean this in a political sense, but a personal one. Gen Z is more concerned with saving money and skeptical of taking on debt than their predeces-sors. They have seen millennials struggling with college debt and stunted careers and are thus making more conservative choices about their finances.

The Coming Work-Life Options

This reserved and practical outlook colors how Gen Z fits work into the fabric of their lives. They are moving beyond work-life integration and pursuing what I would call *work-life options*. They appear to value employment stability more than millennials, and they are very interested in establishing a career with firms that offer professional growth and development. They also use their free time to pursue hobbies and interests that might someday become real careers. This is different than the millennial "slasher" phenomenon. Gen Zers aren't pursuing multiple jobs in order to explore different paths. They are pursuing stable careers while cultivating side projects that could one day become businesses. They take a more entrepreneurial—even mercantilist—approach to their side projects. These are often best described as "side hustles" that, while bringing in a little money now, may someday provide a major source of income. Simon Sinek, author of *Start with Why* talks about how important it is to have a purpose in life. While being a "slasher" or having a "side hustle" will provide the young with opportunities to explore their interests and to make some additional money, more importantly, it will be about discovering something they are passionate about and that gives profound meaning to their lives.

This exploration by Gen Z can be seen clearly with so-called "influencers," young people that build large social media followings and leverage them for corporate marketing dollars. Corporations now spend a significant share of their marketing dollars on paying influencers to use, review, and promote their products. *Business Insider* reported[17] that American companies spent upward of $8 billion on influencer marketing in 2019 and project the annual figure to almost double within three years. The best influencer marketing tends to be the most genuine and organic. Companies now vie to work with influencers that have built genuinely engaged audiences. These young people have found ways to not only develop their personal brand and identity, but to also leverage it into careers. Gen Zers are pursuing all kinds of side hustles, be it as YouTube celebrities or reselling vintage sneakers on eBay.

The side hustle is not just a hobby, and it is not just an exploration of self. The side hustle is a plan B with sights set on plan A. They may have passion for the hustle, but these are also moneymaking efforts that can create a significant revenue stream. I don't mean to paint this group as being obsessed with money— they are merely looking for ways to monetize their interests. They want options, both a stable career *and* an entrepreneurial endeavor. Preferably both will match their personal qualities and bring them fulfillment and financial success.

Of course, not all of these endeavors are so glamorous or focused on the worker. The gig economy has moved much work onto "platforms," such as rideshare apps or task apps such as Task Rabbit, a platform for hiring people to perform typical tasks around the home from raking leaves to running errands. These platforms offer flexibility with a side order of very low pay. However, these gigs do allow workers the flexibility freedom to pursue their actual interests.

---

17 https://www.businessinsider.com/the-2019-influencer-marketing-report-2019-7

Going forward, employers are going to have to adapt to this new perspective on working. Gen Z is going to want greater flexibility to pursue their options. Smart companies will embrace this desire rather than fight against it. Gen Zers are still committed to their job, *for now*, which is the most you can hope for in a transactional labor market. Smart companies allowed millennials to do work their own way—whether it came to the use of tech or the desire for flexible work arrangements—and it should be no different for the new kids on the block. In order to recruit and retain talent, especially in tight labor markets, employers must seek to understand what people want out of work. The young are not lazy or entitled—they simply have a different mindset about how work best fits into life.

Companies and managers must understand that the world has changed, whether they like it or not. Boomers in leadership are beginning to accept that labor markets no longer work the way they once did. Young workers no longer view work in the same way—and they are right not to. The economy has changed, in a transactional labor market, it is incumbent on workers to advocate for their own needs and future.

Given the circumstances, we should not be surprised when employees ask, "What's in it for me?" Or even say, "Here's what I want." In this new work environment, young workers are being upfront about what they want out of work. Know that everyone, regardless of what generational cohort they hail from, would like to have their voices heard and their needs met. Each generation's voice should be welcomed. Some bring wisdom to the table, others experience, others challenge the status quo or offer a fresh perspective. It is through listening to different voices and working with each other that we can meet challenges rather than be polarized by them.

Sometimes, this is about that most precious of all commodities—their time. However, to be quite frank, I am not convinced it is always more time that workers want. The generations' pursuit of different forms of "work-life balance" that looks more like a desire for accommodation, integration, and options suggests that what workers really want is more control over their work lives. They are trying to work in a way that aligns with their personal lives.

Let me be clear: they don't want to work less. They want to make decisions that affect *how* they work. If you love what you do, then when you do it you don't feel as if you are working. According to Mihaly Csikszentmihalyi, the author of *Flow: The Psychology of Peak Performance*, being in flow are those times when an individual is so engaged in what they are doing they lose track of time. And to echo Simon Sinek again from his book *Start with Why*, they want to understand *why* the work is being done in the way that it is. They want autonomy and control over their work lives so that they can make meaningful decisions about the work they do and how it is done. They want to know, in clear terms, what is expected of them and how their performance is being measured.

In other words, they want clear and reasonable parameters and a say in things. Give them these and understand and respect their motivations. Work-life balance will no longer be a battle between work and the rest of life. It never really was. Workers just want to best accommodate, integrate, balance—whatever word you want to use—work into their lives.

The work-life dichotomy was always misleading. Work, when it engages us, it is life affirming. It is part of life. We need to move beyond the notion of a dichotomy, that work is simply the thing we do for a paycheck and "life" merely the momentary reprieves between showing up at the office. Increasing worker engagement would allow us to retire the notion of work-life balance altogether.

In the next chapter, we will examine how to do just that.

Chapter 8: The Future Is Lopsided

"I remind young people everywhere I go, one of the worst things the older generation did was to tell them for twenty-five years, 'Be successful, be successful, be successful' as opposed to, 'Be great, be great, be great.' There's a qualitative difference."

Cornel West

In the last chapter, we saw that different generations approach work-life balance in their own ways. Consequentially, employers are better off empowering workers to more fully integrate work into their lives in ways that better suit them as individuals. Part of this is a matter of maintaining boundaries: allowing workers to keep work at work so that it doesn't bleed into the rest of their time. However, that is only half of the work-life equation.

We cannot just look at how workers spend their time at home. The quality of the time spent at work also matters. If we consider worker engagement as a proxy for the quality of the time spent working, the average worker is not happy with the typical work experience.

Our distaste for work is not inherent. Some people are satisfied and even excited about the work they do—it's just that many are not. There are a number of reasons for this: a bad boss, lack of challenge, inability to advance or achieve promotion, difficult working conditions, a lack of respect, and many other factors. There are as many reasons to be unhappy with work as there are workers. However, the vast majority of these reasons can be reduced down to their ultimate result: a lack of worker engagement.

The workforce is suffering a disengagement crisis. This is not a uniquely American problem. In fact, the United States does better in terms of self-reported engagement than most other developed nations. But we are still failing to keep workers engaged. In 2020, Gallup noted[18] 54% of workers were disengaged and nearly 14% were *actively* disengaged. These workers cost companies real money because they are vocal about their unhappiness. It shows in their work and can drag other workers down as well.

Conversely, engaged workers are those who are enthusiastic about work and committed to the job. They come to work excited and are eager to get—and stay—involved. They are active participants in the success of a company. It is no exaggeration to say that engaged workers carry an organization almost on their own, which is remarkable when you consider that only one in three employees are engaged.

These disengaged workers are not necessarily *bad* workers. They just don't find their work engaging. People aren't born "engaged" or "disengaged." It is mostly a matter of circumstance.

---

18   Jim Harter, "Historic Drop in Engagement Follows Record Rise," Gallup, July 2020.   https://www.gallup.com/workplace/313313/historic-drop-employee-engage-ment-follows-record-rise.aspx

W. Edwards Deming, a leading management thinker in the field of quality who was credited with helping Japan become a manufacturing powerhouse after World War Two, said, "A bad system will beat a good person every time."[19] We should therefore not lay all of the blame for disengagement on the disengaged workers themselves. The situation we face is not just a matter of workers not liking their jobs. While individuals have different interests and strengths that are better suited for certain roles, the sources of disengagement are often structural. This is why management, not the managed, is ultimately responsible for solving the problem. If management took the time to examine the way employees are developed, evaluated, and assigned roles, they would be on the path to solving this issue.

Widespread worker disengagement was much rarer prior to the collapse of the company man model of employment. It may well be an issue of semantics, as employee engagement is a relatively new term. The company man survey equivalent would have been their level of job satisfaction. The distinction between the two, according to Gallup, is that you can be satisfied with your job but at the same time not be emotionally or cognitively engaged. Also, as discussed in previous chapters, workers and employers had a mutual understanding of the employment contract. Be loyal to the company and you will be cared for and rewarded. Vocalizing one's discontent was surely not a sign of loyalty, and it wasn't in one's best interest to do so.

While this covenant was still in place, the biggest driver of job satisfaction was *commitment.* The company man had to be committed or, at the very least, *appear* committed, if he wanted to remain—or ever even become—a company man. Loyalty was

---

19   W. Edwards Deming, https://deming.org/quotes/10091/

what companies were paying for. In those days, companies judged loyalty based on how much you appeared to be willing to sacrifice for the sake of meeting organizational goals. The company man, no matter his current level, garnered respect for staying with the company and doing a good job over time. This kind of loyalty begets some form of engagement almost automatically, as company men had a real stake in the long-term success of the company in the same way that the owners and shareholders did. They weren't going anywhere, and so they had "skin in the game." This made the company man more likely to be committed and thus "loyal."

An important distinction between then and now is this commitment was between the worker and the *organization*, not a particular boss. Where one's loyalty lies has shifted away from the organization to the manager. Today, in the transactional labor market, workers no longer necessarily commit to a company for the long haul. This doesn't hold true for *all* companies, as some companies pride themselves on putting "people first," but the reality for most employees is that the employment contract is transactional. Commitment and the expression of "loyalty" have become more intimate. Workers may commit to good bosses and managers but not necessarily the company. When employees do have positive experiences with multiple bosses over time at the same company, the company's claim of being "people first" may in fact ring true for them. Jim Clifton and Jim Harter, authors of *It's the Manager*, make this point: "The biggest single factor impacting the long-term success of a business is the quality of the managers." What seems to matter to employees today is what is happening to me, the worker, in the here and now. And the manager clearly plays an outsized role in this equation.

As such, it is critical that management and the C-suite work with employees to ensure that they are in the right roles. Workers need to know what they need to do, understand why they are doing it, and believe that they are learning and growing. The very best employees are always going to be the ones who *choose* to be where they are as opposed to feeling that they *have* to be there. Having options makes workers feel like they have more control over their destiny.

And here, a message to all managers out there: I am sorry to break the news to you. Quite often, the blame for disengaged employees lies with *you*. Managers often fail to create engaging work lives for their employees. You, dear managers, are environmental creators. You have the power to create positive workplaces that provide individualized feedback, developmental opportunities, and evaluations focused on developing strengths and minimizing weaknesses. Give your employees what we all want: the sense of accomplishment that comes from knowing that our contributions are important to the success of the business.

It's no wonder that so many workers don't feel engaged. A bad boss and poor management can even negatively impact enthusiastic, positive workers. Caring and supportive management can keep workers engaged in the company and its work. Poor, ill-trained, or hostile management does the opposite. Failing to support employees in doing their job lowers morale, full stop. Low morale does not make for engaged workers.

We workers have continued to show up and do the job, engaged or not. This is a tale as old as business itself. What *is* new is how young workers are now reacting to this status quo. As a boomer, I always accepted this Faustian bargain: I show up and do what I'm told, you pay me. Work is work, right? This is just how things are? When I was working at companies, I would never have deigned to push the envelope. I certainly complained to my colleagues and they to me. (On the bright side, shared misery is a bonding experience.) But we still did what was asked of us. We complied. We weren't necessarily satisfied or engaged, but we did the work anyway. Well, we met the minimum requirements, at any rate.

Moving from simple compliance to commitment requires engagement. But what is engagement? It can be a vague term. Essentially, engagement is a function of how well a worker's talents match the requirements of their specific role. We all have different interests, passions, and preferences when it comes to our work. Certain workers are simply better suited for certain sectors, companies, and roles. While it is true that workers naturally gravitate toward sectors and jobs that interest them, as we tend to study and pursue that which aligns with our interests, the realities of the job market often result in workers making compromises about where they work. We will not all land a dream job pursuing our passions.

We aren't all fit for all roles. I started out studying architecture in college. While I loved architecture, architecture didn't love me. So, I moved into accounting instead. Unfortunately, accounting didn't add up for me either. By the time I graduated, I was majoring in marketing. I was on my third degree before I discovered that my true interest was in how organizations worked, and, more specifically, how we work in organizations. That was the right fit for me; other roles that I tried out were simply not as engaging to me.

This was college, though. When I entered the workforce, I joined a company and *complied*. Young boomers didn't think much about finding deep meaning in our work. We needed to find a job. We applied for jobs that sounded interesting at companies that seemed exciting. However, in the midst of a job hunt, many workers, then and now, are forced to accept the first reasonable offer that comes our way, whether the job is a good fit or not. People need to pay their bills. People need a steady revenue stream.

When a job isn't engaging, however, workers become dissatisfied. Without proper support from employers to help find them a more suitable role, many young workers simply look elsewhere. This is exceedingly common in the modern transactional workplace. When young millennial workers are unhappy with their job or boss, they may simply leave. This is *very* common. According to Gallup, six in ten millennials are open to new job opportunities at any given time. One in five millennials has hopped jobs in the last year.

While boomers are quick to dismiss millennials as flaky for this behavior, these young workers are actually being entirely rational. Why would they stay in a role that doesn't suit them, working for a boss that doesn't support them? Millennials hop jobs in pursuit of what Herminia Ibarra, author and professor of organizational behavior at the London Business School, called "match qualities," which are aspects of jobs that align with a worker's talents, skills, preferences, and interests. This is perfectly reasonable behavior and actually *good* for the overall economy. Companies should be happy that workers are looking for jobs that suit them well. This has been one of the positive impacts of the transactional labor market. The ability for workers to seek out roles that match their personal qualities makes the workforce more efficient and the economy stronger. Companies perform better when employees are well suited to their roles.

This raises the question: In a transactional labor market where workers are free to hop from job to job in search of better "match quality," *why are so many American workers so disengaged at work?*

Unfortunately, the blame (and the onus) often falls on employers. Many companies fail to accurately evaluate and develop their workers in ways that encourage success and, ultimately, engagement. In order to understand how this happens, one must understand lopsidedness.

Enter the Lopsided Worker

Millennials were raised to believe they are *special*. This is where the "generation me" moniker comes from. Many parents raised their millennial children to believe that they could do anything and be anything. Millennials were the first generation to routinely receive awards for participation—for something as simple as just *showing up*. Parents were more realistic and raised their kids to believe that, while they couldn't excel at literally everything, they could excel at *something*. Millennials internalized this message, and they frame their lives, including their work lives, as a search for meaning, self-discovery, and constant, healthy self-improvement. They are trying to find that which makes them special. I personally believe that we are all special and unique in our own way, but—I'm sorry, dear millennials—there is nothing particularly special or unique about being special and unique. Being distinctive is a given, we are all distinctive in our own way. What we are so often missing is being in a place where we can leverage and be recognized for our special and unique distinctions.

While millennials are often maligned for this "specialness" complex, this is actually a neutral generational trait that has some positive impact. To start with, millennials aren't wrong. They *are* special, each and every one of them, as are we all. Every person has positive traits, talents, and abilities. Our specific combination of strengths and weaknesses makes us all unique.

A person is not all strengths, of course. We all also have

weaknesses. We start with certain talents that make us naturally good at some things, not so great at others. The gap between our strengths and weaknesses becomes further delineated over time as we pursue interests, education, training, and on-the-job learning. Any improvement on our weaknesses is often far outpaced by the growth in our strengths. We hone the skills that we are good at and enjoy doing. Our skill sets eventually become our own, but the uneven development of skills makes us ever more lopsided as we advance. This is completely natural and merely the inevitable outcome of focusing on and enhancing our natural innate talents rather than committing to the development in areas where we initially struggled.

Raw talent will only take you so far. Desire is what drives the commitment needed to turn talent into honed skill. Nature can give you a head start by way of talent, but *nurture* is how we develop strengths and eventually, even, how we achieve greatness, even if we weren't so good to start with. Lopsidedness, in this case, is a sign of personal growth and improvement. It is the prioritization and investment in what you think best defines you.

In her book *Different*, Youngme Moon, a professor of business at Harvard Business School, applied the concept of lopsidedness to brands. She noted that most companies pursue the same strategies in pursuit of being all things to all people only to see their products collapse into mediocrity. Brands become generic when they go down this path. There is no perfect combination because a brand cannot be everything to everyone. Those brands that stand out aren't perfect. They are just really good at certain things, which makes them stand out in the market. Smart brands are lopsided in that they focus on certain aspects while intentionally ignoring others. These companies accept that they aren't good at everything. They don't have to be. They are good at some things, which allows them to excel at what they do.

Failing to understand this concept, many companies try to "correct" lopsidedness by shoring up non-essential aspects of their operations and brands, typically to their own detriment. Companies that try to excel at everything do so at the expense of a focus on core business processes. Instead of honing what they are good at and known for, they try to "do it all," generally to no avail. It is very hard to be good at everything. In fact, it's impossible. No one company can be the best at everything. The strongest companies are specialized—they are lopsided—and that's a good thing. They identify and embrace their one competitive anchor. It is inefficient to pursue unnecessary skills. Well-roundedness is not its own virtue.

We stand out by being good at something. Consider some popular automobile brands. Volvo is known for safety, Tesla for being environmentally friendly, and Rolls-Royce, for luxury. They may be good at many things, but we, as consumers, associate them with their most easily identifiable quality, which hopefully, for most automakers, is a strength. The same goes for people. We are not needed or remembered for all that we do, but we are memorable for a few things we do well. Winston Churchill wasn't remembered for his dance moves in the same way Britney Spears is not known for her oration.

Companies should embrace lopsidedness at every level of operations, including human resources. Lopsidedness is a byproduct of specialization and every bit as beneficial to employees as it is to brands. The trick is to have the right combination of specialized workers in roles that play to their strengths. You want good public speakers in public relations, meticulous, detail-oriented people in accounting, and tech-savvy people working over in IT. More importantly, you want people excited about public speaking working in PR, people who want to be detail oriented in accounting, and those who enjoy technology in IT.

While this makes intuitive sense, and any H.R. department worth its salt will hire based on relevant skills, many corporations are not actually *evaluating* those workers on relevant skills alone. The majority of American companies evaluate employees on a number of standardized measures across a broad spectrum of vaguely worded traits or competencies. They are hiring workers with unique skill sets and placing them together on teams or in departments. Teammates should have skill sets and traits that complement each other in working together toward common goals. But this isn't what companies prioritize.

More and more often, you'll see that companies want employees to have skill sets that are interchangeable and redundant, so that they can slot whoever wherever. There are advantages to this in that people can readily fill in for others deemed to have the same skill set. The problem lies with how individuals on teams operate and what is being evaluated. Teams aren't evaluated as teams. Instead, companies evaluate individuals, typically on some informal bell curve that measures their performance across all of their skills. This has team members competing with each other to prove they are in the top 10 percent. Companies should instead reward the best performing teams, not the best team members. Nucor is an example of this philosophy as highlighted in the book, *Humanocracy: Creating Organizations as Amazing as the People Inside Them* by Gary Hamel and Michele Zanini. Among the slew of remarkably innovative processes at Nucor is how the concept of rewarding teams is central to their compensation model. Bonuses at Nucor are paid not to individuals but rather to teams that demonstrate collaboration. Nucor as a company thinks systemically and lives by its motto "We don't build steel we build people."

Evaluating employees by a one-size-fits-all generic rubric incentivizes employees to be either similar or more well-rounded. This means that everyone, even those at the top, dilute their potential by allocating their time and energy to areas that may not be either relevant to the work at hand or are not leveraging their full capabilities in the areas where they could add the greatest value. They spend so much time developing weaknesses that they cannot exploit their full potential. Employees are rewarded for staying ahead of each other according to measures that may not matter rather than for their contribution to meeting team goals.

This practice is a holdover from the days of the company man. When employers were expected to take care of workers for life, they were less likely to fire (and therefore hire) employees. For young boomers, companies didn't simply issue layoffs to rid themselves of workers with obsolete skill sets. It would not have made sense to do so in a time of such extreme economic growth in a tight labor market. Workers could be retrained and moved around as necessary. Companies worked with the talent they had. They would fit loyal employees wherever they could. Whether they actually "matched" the role was not the sole (or even the primary) consideration. *Loyalty was rewarded over match quality*. Thus, the performance evaluation became a necessary tool for determining who would be promoted to the next level. This evaluation process took on something of a formulaic air, but it was still opaque and highly subjective. Good managers have always tried to help employees develop and find positions for them that matched their interests, but in such a siloed and hierarchical business environment, there were only so many ways to shuffle workers around within the company.

This situation had the potential to make employees quite

unhappy. Organizations were rigid and so workers were expected to be flexible. At various points in a career, people were likely to find themselves in positions for which they were ill-suited or lacked "passion." (Passion is a tired, overused, cliché and the source of guilt for workers who probably aren't given control over how they work. "Passionate workers" are often those who can focus on strengths, effectively exercising and being recognized for their lopsidedness.) If the employee felt dissatisfied or disengaged, well, there was little he could do about it as a young boomer. He couldn't easily leave his job. Quitting meant giving up seniority and retirement benefits. He was tied to the company just as much as the company was tied to him.

With the rise of the transactional labor market, these old restraints no longer apply. The current employment landscape is far more uncertain and fluid. Companies no longer hire and promote employees based on loyalty alone. It's job performance that determines one's longevity in a company. Today, management prioritizes performance over loyalty. Gen X knew this, as they saw their fathers downsized or right-sized right out the door after devoting a lifetime to the company. No, Gen X and the generations that followed didn't want loyalty paid back with loyalty. They wanted cold, hard cash, benefits, flexibility, guaranteed time off, stock options, vesting options, and other material rewards. What are you going to do for me? That is the transactional labor market.

The shift toward a transactional labor market has allowed companies to be more flexible with their human resources. They can let go of employees that no longer fit the company rather than being forced to find a place for them. Fewer companies want or need to hire well-rounded workers or promote and develop them organically. They are free to seek out specialized workers that fill a current need. When needs change, they can simply assemble new teams of new workers or tap into the corporate training market suited for building specific sets of discrete skills as needed.

Despite these changes, people in management—particularly we boomers—still expect employees to be endlessly flexible. After all, *we* were. Gen X managers tend to have a similar expectation, albeit for a different reason. They themselves are self-sufficient and will figure out what needs to be done and do it. They expect the same of those they manage.

It is an unfortunate waste of potential that workers are still evaluated on their ability to fit any role rather than their actual critical and value-added contributions. Evaluation systems are often standardized across teams, departments, and even whole companies. This is partly institutional inertia and management's desire to be "fair" with everyone. And to be fair we must have *some* common criteria of evaluation. While well-intentioned, this evaluation system fails to recognize and reward the true talents of employees. It also fails to measure the collective performance of employees in service of organizational goals, and that is what really matters. This evaluation system makes it harder to experiment with different ways to build, retain, and evaluate talent.

Rather than evaluating employees across all variables, companies could evaluate workers on the skills that are actually needed and most valuable in their current roles. Today's knowledge workers are the most specialized workers to ever exist. Modern white-collar work often requires deeper expertise in a narrower range. They should be judged on their *relevant and unique* contributions. This is why lopsidedness will—*must*—become more prevalent. The modern world, the modern business world, is complex. Dealing with complexity is a team sport. It requires deep expertise across a range of topics. We don't ask goalies to be good at driving the puck down the ice. We ask them to safeguard the goal. We don't have to be good at everything, just pretty good at basic things (like, say, ice skating) and really good at certain things that are our hallmark contribution (like, say, blocking shots). Weaknesses brought up to a level of adequacy are fine if they don't keep us from applying our strengths as needed.

Embrace lopsidedness in your workers. Specialized knowledge workers have their own sets of unique abilities and contributions. Recognize them, honor them—not just in yourself but in others—put them to use in the right ways. Stop wasting time and resources trying to force employees to aspire to be good at everything. They cannot—the best they can do is pretend. Slot workers into positions that play to their strengths, where they won't be hindered by their weaknesses. Doing so makes for stronger teams and stronger companies—it also makes for more engaged employees.

Of course, we all have to do some things we don't like or aren't good at. The workplace is dynamic. We aren't cogs or automatons. Sometimes we have to make do and get something done. In those times, it is good to be flexible and adaptive. *But the true value that employees bring to a team is in applying their strengths toward meeting shared goals.* The more time workers spend on *things they both do well and find engaging* the happier and more productive they will be.

Millennials are already looking for positions with better match quality. They approach life as a journey of self-discovery and are looking for positions that align with and bolster their strengths and interests. They will be particularly receptive to employers that recognize their strengths and help move them into roles that match their qualities.

Moving employees into the best positions for them may require restructuring the workplace. Companies would be wise to think systemically. Think of this as a "greenfield site" activity. By way of explanation, a greenfield site is a term used when a manufacturing plant is going to be built from scratch. It allows the company to look at all the processes involved in manufacturing the product. It then designs the plant to maximize both the efficiency of the plant and the quality of the product. If all you had was a *green field*, what could this factory look like? So, start designing from scratch, at least on paper, and pick one area of the company or business. First, perform an inventory of what needs to be accomplished. What are the deliverables and goals for that area of the company? Write them down. Next, determine what tasks must be done to meet those goals and what skills are needed.

Next, take stock of your talent. Determine where they are brilliant and exceptional in their skills and traits. Determine where they are just good enough. Include them in this assessment. Have employees rate themselves and their colleagues on different skills. Finally, design teams of employees who complement one another. The collective should have all the skills necessary to complete the given critical tasks.

Meanwhile, create evaluation metrics for the *team*. Reward the team, not the individuals, as a consequence of the deliverable. Only then—and here's the difficult part—do you have the team decide how to divvy up the rewards. This is where the team—not just you, the manager—evaluates the individual performance of team members. Individuals should be evaluated on how they contributed to the team achieving (or failing to achieve) its goals and deliverables.

I advise at least two levels of evaluation. First, how did the individual perform on the particularly critical areas at which they were asked to contribute? Second, how did the individual do on basic performance, such as reliability, follow-through, and other contributions that the team finds necessary to partner effectively? (These are often basic "people skills," which most people can be taught.) In the spirit of embracing lopsidedness, team members should excel at the first set of evaluations and be merely "good enough" at the second.

Workers do not have to be absolutely brilliant right from the start. They will grow and learn. *The most important thing is that they have talent and a desire to excel at some mission-critical skill that will complement the rest of the team.* Be sure to consider strengths that they may not be using. You might be wasting talent that could be better deployed elsewhere. Don't worry about weaknesses that are irrelevant to their role or those for which others may easily compensate.

In this process, organizations should focus not only on their desired outcomes but also on their employees' needs and desires. Let me be clear: companies do not exist to make their employees happy. Their primary goal is to satisfy their customers' needs at a profit. Businesses are businesses. They need to turn a profit above all else. But ignoring your employees' needs, wants, and humanity is not good for the bottom line—especially for knowledge workers with portable skills that can take their specialized talents elsewhere. It just so happens that happy workers who are engaged in their work make for better employees. Nucor, as mentioned in *Humanocracy,* employs a people-first philosophy and has been continuously profitable since 1969. Engagement is crucial to productivity, efficiency, and effectiveness. Getting the right people into the right positions is crucial to success.

While companies should certainly make the most of their talent, sometimes it will be necessary to let people go. Sometimes, a person's skills and interests no longer fit within a company. Letting them go with grace is as good for them as it is for the company. You do them no favors stringing them along in a role in which they are and will remain unhappy and unproductive. There is almost assuredly the right job for everyone, even if it isn't at your company or on your team. They and the organization will be better served by moving on to an organization and role that better matches their qualities.

Workers who are shown respect, who are afforded dignity, and who are offered a fair understanding of the circumstances are better positioned to go out into the wider economy and find the right position. If the entire labor market operated this way, workers could move in and out of organizations with less friction and animosity. The entire economy functions more efficiently when workers can move freely between companies to find roles that match their talents and interests. This is one of the virtues of the transactional labor market and we should embrace it!

Likewise, show grace and humility when an employee decides to leave. Understand that they are on a search for a job that matches their own, unique qualities. It is not a rebuke of your company or management that they are ready to move on. Just as employers' needs change, so do the needs of workers. Support them in that change and growth and you will find that they speak well of the company going forward.

And who knows, when they are further into their path of self-discovery, they may even "boomerang" back, as more employees are doing. I encourage managers to stay in touch with past employees. Managers are not mere evaluators. Good managers identify, develop, and nurture talent. By acting as a mentor and confidante for employees, past and present, you build rapport and clout in your industry.

Does this sound hard? Well, I'm sorry to say that yes, it is hard, at first . . . but once managers start to consistently consider the needs and wants of employees in the transactional labor market, it will develop into a healthy habit. Companies that treat employment as a one-way street do so at their own risk—and at their own peril. Young knowledge workers with portable skill sets will simply up and leave if their needs aren't being met. Highly sought-after, experienced workers do it all the time in this new labor market.

Millennials and Gen Zers want to be treated with humanity and respect from the get-go. They want to exercise and develop their skills in positions that play to their strengths. They want to work for management that recognizes their contributions and values their opinions. Employers that recognize these desires and work to slot workers into the right roles, treat them right, keep them engaged, and nurture their development will build the strongest teams and most profitable organizations.

Do What You Enjoy, Enjoy What You Do

Embracing lopsidedness and helping workers develop their strengths will help them become engaged, but it will not happen overnight. Engagement is difficult for many young workers because they are still in the discovery process. Older millennials have a clearer sense of themselves, and thus a clearer sense of their strengths, weaknesses, and interests as they have had a variety of experiences and opportunities to develop them. Gen Z might have inclinations and interests; but for something to become a *strength*, proficiency and practice are required. These young workers may still need time to develop their talents.

As I mentioned in a previous chapter, in his book *Flow*, Mihaly Csikszentmihalyi defines "flow" as total immersion in an activity. In a state of flow, the doer is one with the doing. It is a state of complete and total engagement. In such a state, work no longer even seems like work. Flow is the ultimate work-life balance—it is the complete and total integration of work and self. If we could remain in a state of flow at all times, a debatable notion to be sure, all of the challenges associated with the concept of work-life balance that we've discussed in the previous chapter would be moot. Work would just be another engaging (and even pleasurable) activity, not so different from leisure or pursuing hobbies. There would not be any need to balance work against the rest of life—it would simply be another, fully-integrated *aspect* of life, rather than something to be endured or withstood until it's time to go home. While doing something engaging, humans do not dwell on what they would rather be doing. They actually *become* part of the doing.

For some people, this is more or less a sustainable reality. Some people find their jobs totally engaging. Many people find at least some parts of their jobs satisfying. As a public speaker, I enter a state of flow when stepping onto a stage and speaking to a friendly and engaged audience . . . or, at least, I *imagine* they are. I get so involved in speaking to my audience that everything else disappears into the background. It becomes just the audience and me. I am totally immersed in that moment. I can only hope the feeling is mutual. It is fun and rewarding. I can hardly call it work. It really doesn't feel like work. Much of my time working "on stage" is the most enjoyable and engaging part of my professional journey. This is the part of my work I am most likely to wax poetic about with others. When I get up on stage, I enter a state of flow and time disappears as I become one with what I am doing.

This doesn't happen for everyone, not right away. The more seasoned among us forget what it is like to be a beginner. This is one reason why boomers struggle to understand why younger workers are so disengaged. Seasoned professionals often advise the young to "do what you love." While sound advice, the people offering it forget or fail to realize that they themselves are coming from a place of mastery and, hopefully, contentment. With experience and focus comes mastery. We get better at things the longer that we do them. Mastery begets satisfaction. We are more likely to love that which we have embraced, mastered, and conquered. Seasoned professionals grow to love what they do. When they advise the young to just "do what you love," they do so based on insights gained from a lifetime of doing the work. They do so from a place of mastery, in which they can achieve flow and become easily engaged in the work. Engagement is simply easier when you are good at something, and it is easier to be good at something when you have spent countless hours perfecting it.

For the master, the work comes easy, as if by virtuosity. For the neophyte, hard work just seems hard. The struggle can actually be painful and laborious, which makes it much harder to enter a state of flow. "Do what you love" may be well-intentioned advice, but young people need a path toward proficiency and eventual mastery, not platitudes and aphorisms.

This is all self-reinforcing. Proficiency leads to engagement. As we become more engaged, we become more dedicated to further improvement. Employers can jumpstart this cycle and perpetuate it by providing the optimal conditions for their workers. Engaged workers understand why they are doing something, not just how to do it, because they care about the work. They understand how their work contributes to the greater good. They are developing skills and applying their talents to achieve clear outcomes, which is immensely satisfying. Help workers develop their skills and encourage growth and improvement. Acknowledge when they are making progress. Encouraging progress helps people move from neophyte to mastery.

Unfortunately, some seasoned workers in leadership do not believe it is incumbent upon them to keep their workers engaged. Some of the boomers reading this right now are scoffing, if not recoiling. "You like your job? Great! You don't? Too bad. Work isn't supposed to be fun. That's why it's called *work*! They may be thinking "No one is going to pay you for the things that you want to do."

Of course, this is objectively untrue. Many people get paid for work they find fun or engaging, and not just people with glamorous jobs in media, sports, or entertainment. All kinds of jobs can be engaging when they match up with a person's personal qualities and proclivities. Modern knowledge jobs involve some of the most fascinating and engaging work possible—if you have the temperament for it. Other people enjoy working with their hands. Some are deeply engaged by even repetitive tasks, often reporting entering a calming, meditative state of Zen. But what these people share in common is a deep affinity for the work and a proficiency at it—two things that go hand in hand.

The potential tragedy of a boomer experience is that so many of *them* may not be engaged in their work. While some boomers are engaged at work, having spent a lifetime mastering it, others found themselves in the wrong roles. Unfortunately, while ascribing to this "that's why they call it *work*" philosophy, they never made moves to find meaningful and engaging work, or never thought it would be allowed or even possible. They may have not done anything about their situations because they believed that there was nothing to be done. This may be a generational trait unique to boomers. Boomers were raised to see work as a necessity that one does in order to support one's self and raise a family. While they are free to see the world as they so choose, I would suggest that this perspective is self-limiting. It is also likely to result in unhappiness as one is simply resigned to the status quo.

Furthermore, it is making *other people* unhappy too. Boomers still run many American workplaces, and if leadership is not open to entertaining the idea of embracing lopsidedness and rewarding teams they will one day be at a competitive disadvantage relative to companies that do embrace these concepts.

In a transactional labor market, where young workers are always free to look for greener pastures, workplaces need to be more adaptive. Thank God for the arrival of our most adaptive generation, Gen X. As they are now moving into senior management positions, Gen X is more willing and able to question existing organizational structures and experiment with new ones.

But what will this mean for boomers still in the workplace?

The Boomer Legacy

The plus side is boomers are well-situated to make changes to the workplaces they oversee. Many of them—men *and* women—are leading teams across the country and heading up many of our biggest corporations. They have the power to start redefining work and the workplace to make it more engaging. Rather than simply dismissing the young, they can do what their Gen X protégés are doing, which is asking the hard questions about why so many workers are not engaged. Sure, maybe *some* workers might be a bit unfocused or uninspired. But maybe they are in a role that doesn't play to their strengths? Maybe they aren't being challenged? Maybe they don't think management is supporting them? As we have seen in this chapter, there are many structural reasons why the system trumps the individuals working in it. This must change.

Boomers can lead here—and they should. Right now, as the most seasoned generation still in the workplace, we boomers have a claim to the shape of the American workplace. Given that over two-thirds of the workforce report being disengaged at work, is this the legacy for which we want to be remembered? Someday, the "Okay, boomer" meme may be recognized as the first salvo against us from aggrieved younger workers who blame us for the difficulties they are facing.

We boomers are leading younger workers and there is still plenty of time to address these issues. Half of our cohort group is still working. We are also potential role models in this phase of our working lives, which is all the more reason that our optimistic, team-spirited, doggedness is understood and hopefully appreciated by those who follow. For many people lucky enough to have children, they are our legacy. But what kind of world have we created for them? What kind of workplaces? What kind of perspective are they inheriting from us?

Those who subscribe to the "that's why they call it *work*" crowd are failing the next generations in this regard. We would not treat our own children this way. We would not tell them to "just deal with it." We raised our millennial children to pursue their wants and dreams, to insist on understanding why, to work well with others—but then when other people's millennial children come into our workplaces, we shrug (or scoff) and say, "This is the way it is."

We boomers had no intention of deliberately causing any harm, of course. We are simply displaying a generational trait that is born of our upbringing. Boomers were told not to complain about work and so they recoil when younger workers with little experience do so. They often see millennials as entitled for simply making requests or asking questions. Some boomers find this offensive. They believe that, if the world as it is was good enough for them, well then it is good enough for you "youngins," too.

This is hardly the path to a better future. Boomers in leadership should cultivate workplaces that work for workers, especially as we prepare to hand the reigns over to the next generation. Rather than reminding the younger generations of how things "used to be," we boomers should be trying to understand how younger generations *want* things to be—and then helping them achieve that better reality. We won't be in the workplace forever—why shouldn't the workplace of the future accommodate those who will actually be working in it?

While we boomers can facilitate the creation of the workplaces of the future, we cannot create them alone. Thankfully, the leadership transition will involve passing the baton to a set of very adaptive Gen Xers and millennials that have moved up the ranks. We can work with them to solve the engagement crisis. Boomers have institutional and "cultural" knowledge about how companies or firms *really* operate. Most firms are like icebergs, the policies and stated procedures are above water but the actual behaviors and actions it takes to succeed are below. These unwritten rules are opaque and difficult to discern for recent arrivals. Collaborating with younger cohorts to surface the rules and to imagine different ways of working will require engagement across all generations. Everyone has a stake in the outcome and a unique contribution to make in achieving it.

I, for one, do not want my legacy—or the legacy of my generation—to be the material wealth we have created. Working hard is in our generational mantra. Being deferential to authority and doing the work, whatever the work may be, is how we were raised. But if I may offer boomers another thought: *We should be working smarter, not harder.* Our most precious commodity is time. Spending time on unfulfilling, mindless work that doesn't suit our preferences is a *waste* of time. Working in a stifling, thankless environment with no sense of autonomy or self-destination is a tragedy.

And so, we are at a fork in the road. Do we leave work as we found it? Or do we experiment with new and perhaps more stimulating and rewarding work environments where people are allowed to embrace the work that they enjoy? I suggest we work to build something better in our remaining years at work. And, by remaining years, I mean of course the next two or three decades, I am a boomer after all.

Chapter 9: Resuscitating the Performance Review

"The single biggest problem in communication is the illusion that it has taken place."

George Bernard Shaw

Feedback is an integral part of the workplace experience, and it manifests itself in many forms. Feedback can be positive/reinforcing or negative/redirecting. It can be structured or informal. Feedback can come from a client, be shared among peers, or be delivered from a supervisor to her direct report. In its highest and best use, feedback is a constructive nudge that sparks awareness, action, and improvement. The ways in which feedback is sent and received—its effectiveness or lack thereof —are heavily influenced by the generational dynamics at play between sender and receiver. In this chapter, we will examine a feedback mechanism that is as common as it is ineffective. Our object lesson: the annual performance review.

Feedback is helpful in developing one's skills and talents and is essential to optimizing performance. Historically, supervisors gave formal feedback through an annual performance review. Employees took in the feedback and adjusted their behavior. This approach has been applied to individuals in organizations over the decades so one might assume this is an effective model. One fundamental flaw in the system is the most specific and relevant feedback is given to the worst-performing employees. Generally, this is not an attempt at reformation but rather the creation of a paper trail to justify an inevitable separation. The problem children get the most attention. More recently, some organizations have broadened their focus to include the rising stars. Processes to identify, retain, and nurture the highest potential employees (or "Hi-Po's") have grown in popularity. This is progress but a glaring omission remains. The missed opportunity lies between the extremes as the majority of employees fall in the middle ground known as "good." Very few performance review systems are geared to providing worthwhile feedback to help the good become great.

Millennials make up the largest generational cohort in the American workforce. The flaws in the annual review process are readily apparent to millennials and Gen Zers, both of which have been raised to expect regular doses of substantive feedback. A more effective, holistic, and collaborative approach is needed.

Before I become prescriptive and make suggestions for both the senders and receivers of feedback, I think it is important to look at feedback and the evaluation process from an historical perspective. What follows is an overview of my close encounters with the annual performance review. We will then explore why this clearly inadequate system has enjoyed such tremendous staying power across Corporate America. I will close with a rather progressive suggestion for a new model that increases feedback receptivity particularly for millennials and Gen Zers.

One Boomer's Personal Introduction to Feedback

As a young professional in my first "adult" job, I underwent many of the corporate world's rites of passage. The most anticlimactic of them was my first annual performance review. It consisted of a fifteen-minute meeting with my supervisor in which he read a summary of my performance from a one-page file he could just as easily have handed to me. I remember little of what was said. He might have had a minor suggestion or two, but nothing notable. My performance was deemed sufficient and that was that. There was more gossip about who was or wasn't promoted than actual discussion of my performance. Once a respectable amount of time had passed, we adjourned. There was no follow-up. It would be another 365 days before we revisited anything that had been discussed in the review. The act was perfunctory; a rote exercise that neither encouraged nor facilitated further discussion.

This feedback experience was typical for the times. The annual performance review was a ritualistic formality. We weren't necessarily receiving feedback on our performance or working toward improvement. We were being judged on a binary. You were either "okay" or "falling short." There was hardly any in-between. It was pass/fail. If you passed, you kept your job and maybe got a bonus or salary raise if they were handing them out that year. If you failed, you might want to start polishing that resume.

For the most part, we already knew which camp we belonged

to well before the actual performance review. If you were falling short on the job, your supervisors would have made this abundantly clear *on the job*. Everyone else could assume they were in the "okay" camp. Unfortunately, during our performance reviews, our supervisor-taskmasters did not provide us with much by way of actionable feedback. We would get a pat on the back and be told to keep up the good work.

I came to realize that the performance reviews may have been *about* us, but they weren't *for* us. They were a managerial tool, rarely leveraged to give real performance-enhancing feedback. The performance review had the biggest impact on people who were already on the path to the point of no return. For these unfortunate souls, a performance review was management's way of getting the ball rolling on termination. The rest of us simply got an annual nod of approval. A positive performance might be retroactively cited as the reason for a raise, bonus, or promotion, assuming these things were on the table at all. For most of us, most years, it was a formality. Our fates were already sealed before we sat down and went through the motions.

Whether one had earned an "okay" or "falling short" rating, the news came well before the performance review. We were told how we were doing on the job, albeit in a rather skewed way. The feedback was not balanced. Our supervisors were quick to let us know when we were messing up. They would bark at us or, in my own experience, throw furniture (I kid you not) when mistakes were made. This kind of corrective feedback was immediate and pointed, if not always diplomatic. We rarely received substantive positive feedback on the job. We might have gotten an "Attaboy!" when something went well on our watch.

There are a few reasons for this discrepancy between positive and negative feedback. First, we were entry-level neophytes that had just been hired onto the team. We really *were* making mistakes that needed to be corrected. With plenty of low-hanging fruit and easy gains, our supervisors were quick to call out blunders. Second, it is human nature to correct mistakes. We naturally take notice when we see someone doing something wrong. The mistakes we made were ultimately attributed to our supervisors, giving them a natural incentive to step in and get us to do things the right way. However, there were no direct or immediate consequences for failing to call out our strengths or acknowledge what we were doing correctly.

Those of us who were mostly doing a good job still only received feedback in the form of a thumbs-up or thumbs-down. It was good to know when we were doing something wrong or right, but our evaluators simply issued the conclusion and attached a numeric rating to it. We had no way of knowing the specific behaviors we had exhibited that led to these conclusions. Eventually, we would lose interest in what was supposed to be a skill-building or reinforcing process. It was like bowling with a curtain. You could hear pins falling, but you don't know which pins. Who'd want to bowl ten frames that way?

———

This feedback was not prescriptive. It didn't tell us what we should be doing *instead*. The "needs improvement" or, conversely, the "attaboys" did not offer guidance. We knew the general direction of the feedback, but not how to get *better*. Young boomers—like me—had to rely on ourselves to figure out what we were doing wrong and adjust our behavior accordingly. Without clear guidance, we had to guess. Those of us who guessed the right answer often enough became masters of the game called office politics, something that later generations abhor.

Why the Performance Review as We Know It Just Won't Die

Despite the shortcomings listed above, the old-school performance review enjoys incredible staying power. Some workers insist upon them, partly out of inertia and partly because it is better than nothing. Boomers are accustomed to this kind of "feedback," no matter how limited its value. Some news is better than no news, and we accept performance reviews as just the way things are. Those of us who have been in our fields and positions for decades don't always need frequent or thorough feedback, which makes a quick "check the box" review appealing. This kind of review may be appropriate to those who have mastered the skills relevant to their work, but those employees who are still on the learning curve deserve so much more.

One could mount a defense of the performance review as an internal managerial tool: it is efficient and provides a sense of (at least perceived) meritocracy. I won't argue the matter one way or the other. If used effectively, the performance review *could* be a method for delivering employees relevant, balanced, and actionable feedback. However, it has been failing terribly at these functions for over half a century. Authors Marcus Buckingham and Ashley Goodall in their book *Nine Lies About Work* challenge many of the existing notions about the use of performance appraisals. Among the many interesting questions that they explore is, "Why is it a settled truth that your manager can reliability rate you on your performance, when on actual teams, none of us has ever met a team leader blessed with perfect objectivity?" *Instead*, the performance review has merely put colleagues into competition over promotions. This might have some considerable value if the review was an accurate reflection of performance in a job, but as we saw when discussing lopsidedness, these reviews tend to focus on being well-rounded rather than well matched to the person in the position.

Despite this persistence, the performance review's days might now be numbered. A growing number of Gen Xers and millennials have joined Boomers in the ranks of leadership. We may well see them do away with the performance review (as some companies have done), which have never suited their needs. Gen X is independent and self-sufficient while millennials are collaborative and inquisitive. The performance review is authoritarian, highly subjective, and sub-optimizing in the valuing of employee contributions. It's a bad match for the new workforce. Before we consider the possibility that millennials may do away with the performance review in favor of some more effective and progressive form of feedback, we must first consider why Gen X failed to do so.

Why Gen X Played Along

Gen Xers are an independent cohort, and competent Gen Xers have little interest in a sugarcoated summary of what they did well over the course of the year. They already know if they did a good job. They aren't interested in feedback as opinion or slap-on-the-back affirmations. They want to know *what* needs doing and how specifically they could do it better. Give them the task, the tools, and the deadline, and let them get to work already. If you have a problem with their work, they want to know in real time. The only feedback they are interested in is timely, pragmatic, and delivered in plain English. Tell a Gen Xer they should have spent the past year doing something differently, and they will want to know why in the hell you didn't say so back in January.

Ever the skeptics, I suspect Gen Xers have long known that the performance review is a bit of a sham. They don't take this kind of feedback seriously because they understand that it is a managerial tool, just another layer of bureaucracy. Then why didn't Gen X do away with the performance review? Gen Xers began transitioning to upper management and executive jobs long ago. Some entrepreneurial Gen Xers left corporate America altogether and founded the technology companies that collectively forged the dot-com boom in the nineties. These were some of the most cutting-edge companies of the day, run by relatively young Gen Xers that had free range to reinvent the corporate structure. In many areas, they did just that. But, by and large, they continued to handle feedback and evaluations in the same old ways. Many administer traditional performance reviews to this very day.

But why?

Like so much to do with generational attitudes and choices, the answer lies in Gen X's childhood. Being a smaller cohort than the boomers and millennials that bookended them, Gen X experienced tighter generational waves and therefore a somewhat more uniform experience. Pretty much all of Gen X grew up in the era of the latchkey kid. They were doing chores unsupervised and generally figuring things out on their own.

These early experiences of fending for themselves instilled Gen X with that sense of self-sufficiency and independence mentioned earlier. They were those "free rangers" who were on their own a lot.

They had free range of not just the house, but also the neighborhood. There was always an unsupervised house available, and this is where small groups of Gen X kids spent much of their time. Many of these kids were spending more time with friends than with family.

Taken as a whole, these factors meant that Gen X wasn't receiving much day-to-day feedback as children. Their parents had bigger things to worry about, especially parents of the early Gen Xers who came of age during the recessions of the seventies and early eighties. Times were difficult and parents were stretched thin. There were no cellphones, much less in-home security cameras, and it wasn't easy for working parents to keep tabs on their kids. Children were being raised by their peers as much as their parents. Unfortunately, kids don't always give the most constructive feedback.

I don't mean to imply that their parents had no rules or standards. Of course, they did. They simply weren't around to offer their children "constant" feedback that for later generations became "concerted cultivation." They were forced to set parameters and allow their young Gen X children some latitude. There was accountability, ultimately, when mom or dad came home. If chores weren't done, there might be hell to pay. But no one was standing over the shoulders of the young Gen X telling them how to do things.

This free-range upbringing taught Gen X to get things done without much external feedback, good or bad. Though stereotyped as loathing authority, Gen X is not so much defiant but rather agnostic to it. If they didn't need someone staring over their shoulder as children—they certainly didn't later as adults with professional jobs and years of experience under their belts.

So why hasn't Gen X revolted against the performance review? Ironically, their disinterest in feedback is precisely what allowed the performance review to survive. For those who don't value the feedback mechanisms in place, the performance review is rather painless. It may induce some eye-rolling, but it's over quickly and easy to ignore. Not needing or waiting for this summary judgment of their performance over the past year, Gen Xers don't particularly mind the shortcomings of the performance review. They never really required feedback unless it related directly to building their skills. They didn't need or want much affirmation beyond tacit approval, which the performance review provided. They wanted to get back to what they were doing before you interrupted them to tell them that they were doing the job right. They already knew that—it's why they were doing it that way!

Why Millennials Don't Play Along

Millennials were raised differently. While their Gen X predecessors were perceived as aloof, this new cohort entering the workplace displayed a seemingly bottomless appetite for attention. The difference between the two generations was so stark that millennials were immediately labeled as too needy. They *seemed* to require constant feedback and affirmation, not to mention an open discussion on how the job they were hired to do should be done.

Boomers found this attitude both grating and disconcerting. They never had to deal with this from Gen X, who neither craved nor wanted affirmation and simply did the job without having to discuss it. Boomers and Gen X seemed fine with this situation, happy to either issue a performance review or be the recipient of one once a year or so and move on. Why were millennials making the performance review, once so efficient and easy, such a problem? Boomers wanted millennials to be more like everyone else in the workplace—accepting of the status quo. Gen Xers wanted the same. They couldn't relate to millennials' "constant" need for details about their performance, both good and bad. Being self-sufficient, Gen X as an employer (not as a parent) wanted millennials to "buck up" and figure things out on their own too.

The irony here is that boomers and the first wave of Gen X were the ones who raised millennials to be this way. They raised their children with an Engage-Discuss mentality, as we saw in previous chapters, which encouraged them to be inquisitive and assertive. Boomers didn't want their children to be stifled as they had been. And Gen X didn't want their children to grow up isolated and operating independently of their families. That is why they so diligently nurtured their millennial children and, as a consequence of their upbringing, working young people can't and don't accept the perfunctory performance appraisal process as it stands today. The parents taught their millennial children to ask questions and engage in open communication. They have never been "needy" unless one is defining needy as the need to know, "Why?"

Unfortunately, this thoughtful nurturing only extended to their *own* children. When millennials entered the workplace, boomers and Gen X found other people's millennial children rude, insubordinate, and entitled for exhibiting these behaviors. They may have wanted their own children to be inquisitive and engaged, but they'd rather yours just do their job without asking too many questions or making too many demands. The reality is they probably didn't view these off-putting employees as young adults who were raised as their own children were raised. Rather, as younger versions of themselves with supposedly the same wants and needs they had when they were in that position.

But millennials *won't* be put off—it's not in their nature. They want more than the occasional affirmation of a job well done. They want real feedback they can use to perform better. They want to know the specifics of how they are being evaluated. They want to be active participants in their own improvement plans. On each and every one of these fronts, the performance review is not making the grade.

Millennials need real, behaviorally based feedback relevant to the work they are doing, delivered in close proximity to the time in which they are doing it. We should happily give it to them. There's nothing wrong with the performance review as a managerial tool, but we need to develop new methods of issuing relevant, actionable feedback.

Strengths-Based Feedback for Strong Workers

The performance review only really succeeds as a managerial tool but fails to provide *good* workers with the pointed advice that would help them become *great* workers.

The reasons for this are largely structural and likely impossible to solve solely by tweaking the performance review. Large organizations tend to evaluate employees on a bell curve, at least informally, often explicitly. The vast majority of workers fall in the middle of the curve, which represents about 80 percent of employees. These workers are competent. They are deemed good at their jobs or, at least, good enough. Those at the top of the bell curve are deemed exceptional but rare. Those at the bottom are the underperformers.

This failure to give constructive feedback to competent workers is why so few workers ever move from good to great. The majority of people are good at their jobs, which is why they got hired in the first place. However, the law of averages dictates that it is hard to become a *great* performer, especially when being evaluated on a bell curve. Going from good to great is never easy.

This is a problem not just for workers, but also for their employers. Organizations can get the much bigger bang for their buck in terms of performance improvement by focusing on the great majority of competent workers worth retaining and investing in. But right now, generally speaking, they are not doing so. Extra efforts are typically made on behalf of the "high performers," which consist of the upper 10 percent of the bell curve as determined by a less than objective evaluation system that contains any number of biases.

In order to provide actionable feedback to these good employees that make up the majority of the workforce, evaluators need to start explaining the "why" of their conclusions. If, for instance, a manager tells an employee they need to be a better team player, that's a conclusion but there is nothing actionable about the statement per se. Millennials get frustrated because managers aren't actually saying how they reached that conclusion. Workers need to know more than the fact that they are meeting expectations. Rather than just providing affirmation, feedback should reinforce helpful behaviors by pointing them out so that workers can focus on doing more of what they are doing right. Ken Blanchard, a noted author and authority on management, summed it up with the title of one of his many books, *Catch People Doing Something Right*.

Clearly, not all feedback is positive, nor should it be, of course. We all have room for improvement, especially when we are developing our skills. Even the best workers should be receiving feedback on what they could be doing better. As we discussed in previous chapters, all people are lopsided in their skills. We are good at some things and less good at other things. Effective feedback will address both strengths and weaknesses. Unfortunately, evaluators often fall victim to the halo effect when it comes to especially talented workers, or its opposite—the horns effect—if the manager has found a particularly glaring fault with an employee. These are cognitive biases that cause exceptionalism in one area to positively influence the perception of other unrelated areas. The halo effect can mask weaknesses, just as the horns effect can mask strengths. If those weaknesses are in areas that are relevant to the role, talented employees may never get feedback that could help them address these deficiencies.

The majority of feedback should focus on people's strengths. This is the kind of feedback that can move a worker's performance from good to great. The 80 percent of workers whose performance falls in the middle of the bell curve are already competent. The majority of feedback they get should be focused on further developing their strengths. Contrary to popular belief and intuition, the most potential for growth lies, in our strengths, not our weaknesses.

Marcus Buckingham and Donald O. Clifton popularized this notion with their book *StrengthsFinder*, which advises workers to identify their strengths and pursue careers that play to them. People that do so are your good workers. Getting them to great is a matter of perfecting those strengths and honing their skill sets to mastery. Feedback should not be focused on shoring up weaknesses that are irrelevant to their positions, but instead, it should focus on what they actually do. Most workers are already pretty good at what they do. Embrace their lopsidedness rather than wasting time and energy on training skills that are irrelevant to a specific role. Hire workers into positions in which they are capable or have an interest in becoming competent and then provide feedback that will help them excel in those roles. In the following chapter, I will also look at how evaluation and rewards must move beyond individuals to include teams and how this notion of embracing lopsidedness will contribute to a team's performance.

It's also important to establish an environment conducive to receiving feedback. No feedback and people feel uneasy. No positive feedback and they feel discouraged and unappreciated. No constructive, actionable feedback and they have no impetus to improve. Note, however, that critical feedback should be constructive and delivered in a way that promotes open dialogue. Workers want to be corrected appropriately when they aren't performing as they should be. They also want to feel supported. There is no need to crack the whip when good employees feel heard, respected, and part of the process. They should also feel safe responding to feedback, which needs to be a collaborative process. Evaluators should be working with employees to help them improve.

Some of you following along on this exploration of generational dynamics are parents (I am confident that *all* of you are someone's children). As parents, you likely already possess the core skills for providing effective feedback. If you, like many middle-class Americans, are raising your children in a manner consistent with the tenets of "concerted cultivation" you already know how to engage your millennial and Gen Z progeny. Leverage the dialogue skills you have used and honed over the years with your own children, and you will be engaging your younger colleagues in a way that is congruent with their own upbringing. Conversely, younger cohorts are already prepared and willing to engage older workers in this manner whether they report to them or, in some instances, if they are managing them. This approach recognizes that the feedback is part of a larger dialogue with the intent of developing their skills and innate talents, moving them and the organization from good to great.

Leveraging Millennial and Gen Z Assertiveness in Getting Feedback

Millennials and their younger cohort, Gen Z, were both raised under a model of parenting that encourages the young to be assertive and inquisitive. I recommend leveraging millennials and Gen Zers's natural assertiveness and curiosity by using what I have termed "collaborative pattern-recognition (CPR) feedback," which can help "breathe a little life into" your feedback and organization, so to speak. As the name suggests, CPR feedback is both collaborative and focused on identifying patterns of behavior.

This is a proactive process that puts the employees in control of getting specific feedback in areas of interest to them. They become active participants, shaping the scope and nature of their own evaluations. This approach encourages them to ask for feedback. While evaluators can ask what a given employee wants feedback on, it is important that the person seeking the feedback ultimately decides where to focus the conversation.

Evaluators should collaborate with workers to identify strengths, as well as relevant weaknesses, and collectively devise a development plan. Rather than handing down feedback from on high, evaluators must involve workers in the process. Workers know themselves better than anyone else. They know how their personal qualities do and do not match the role. Engaging them in dialogue can highlight areas of interest that evaluators may have been totally unaware of. Evaluator and employee are best positioned to make real improvements by working together.

The performance review—with its Tell-Do, one size fits all nature—is at odds with the way millennials would prefer to handle workplace feedback. This is an area in which we should unequivocally defer to their preferences: collaborative feedback is better for everyone that wants to improve in areas that are of interest and relevant to them. I want to issue this challenge to all employers: stop handing summary, conclusive evaluations from on high and instead implement practices that actively engage workers in the feedback process. Evaluation is a reflective activity—it works best when the person being evaluated engages in self-reflection. Work with employees by asking them to think about the projects and work they have done and what it took them to do it.

The organization can then help employees get specific feedback on relevant skills from the very people they work with every day. Collaborative Pattern Recognition feedback should involve not just the worker, but those with whom they work most closely. First, have employees and their supervisors identify those skills and traits that are relevant. Ignore weaknesses that are irrelevant to the job. Then, the employee identifies people within the organization that can assess their performance in these areas. These people should not be limited to just supervisors. We work closely with people at the same level every day. These people often know us and our work. Fellow team members can provide insights that supervisors may miss. They will, as a group, be best suited to evaluate the employee most fully and accurately.

Setting a collaborative tone upfront is critical. Not only will it prevent offense or resentment, but teams will also function better. Allowing team members to give feedback to each other in a safe environment builds camaraderie. The main role of evaluators is to facilitate the feedback process. Ensure that everyone understands the goal is to help each other go from good to great. Keep the developmental feedback mostly focused on strengths. The greatest room for improvement lies in areas where employees are already competent or desire to be one day.

Feedback based on pattern recognition, as CPR is, needs to focus on one competency at a time. This has to do with the nature of the human brain. In his book *The Mind is Flat*, Professor Nick Chater discusses experiments on pattern recognition. The human brain is predisposed to recognize patterns. This is how we make sense of what we see and hear. However, according to Chater, we are limited to only recognizing a single pattern at a time. In order to make CPR effective, the employee seeking feedback should narrow the scope of the request to a single competency.

Once you have identified a competency of interest, make sure that you are working with an adequate data set. Getting multiple sources of feedback is of limited utility if it isn't broad and thorough. Most feedback can be boiled down to one of three types: that which asks you to start, stop, or continue doing something. Asking coworkers and supervisors to provide feedback on what you should *continue* doing, what you should *quit* doing entirely, and what, if anything, you should *start* doing ensures that you have relevant feedback.

The employee and not the evaluator or supervisor collects and analyzes the raw data. With this data in hand, you can start to look for *patterns* in order to separate the signal from the noise. Competent workers are unlikely to see consensus in feedback—that typically happens to workers with obvious problems. Most workers are good at their jobs and will see a variety of suggestions, some of them conflicting. However, with enough good data, patterns and trends will emerge. Look for suggestions or concerns that are repeated. You may consider minority opinions, but you will have to set some aside and that's okay. Again, separate the signal from the noise. This process will leave each employee with a synthesis of the best feedback. The worker can now discuss any patterns with the supervisor and/or coworkers and devise a plan to address recurrent issues and thoughtfully improve upon strengths.

It is critical that everyone involved understands that the intention of the CPR process is to embrace lopsidedness and improve on strengths. When the evaluator knows that the person seeking feedback truly wants to move from good to great, they will feel safe in sharing suggestions and constructive criticism even if the worker is already quite competent.

Collaborative pattern-recognition feedback appeals to millennials because it is congruent with their Engage-Discuss mindset. It appeals to their sense of individuality and self-discovery. CPR appeals to everyone's innate desire for mastery and feedback on how well we are doing the things that we find engaging. We want to work with evaluators to get better at that which interests us. A collaborative evaluation that produces individualized, actionable, data-driven feedback in a safe environment is simply preferable to the unhelpful, nonspecific, vague, and often *absent* feedback that seasoned workers have merely become accustomed to. Like all new things, the process might be strange and uncomfortable at first, but the current feedback model employed by most organizations is simply ineffective for all but the lowest-performing workers.

Nonetheless, some workers may balk at these changes. Gen X, being self-sufficient and ever skeptical, may be particularly resistant to collaborative feedback. Boomers may resist change simply out of inertia. Also, depending on skill level, some boomers and Gen Xers may have achieved such a level of mastery that any honest feedback really will be a simple affirmation. (Having said that, most of us would benefit from hearing good things about what we enjoy doing at work.) Gen Xers may actually find this kind of feedback uncomfortable at first. Unlike millennials, these grownup latchkey kids prefer to figure things out on their own. They are naturally private and perhaps hesitant to discuss their strengths and weaknesses openly with others.

To encourage the adoption of these new methods, it is best to emphasize the self-directed nature of CPR feedback. Feedback of any kind requires taking input from others, even the traditional performance review. CPR feedback at least allows the employee to control the process. They get to identify their own strengths, select the evaluators, analyze the feedback, and collaborate in the development of an improvement plan. The ability to direct the process will appeal to Gen X, even if they have to suffer through other people offering suggestions about how to do their job, which they are already doing anyway, thank you very much! At the very least, most will find the process both more tolerable and more useful, if you can convince them to come to it with an open mind.

Habits are hard to break, but some habits need breaking. The more workers engage in this kind of feedback, the more they will see its virtues, even with those aloof, distant, remote, and cold Gen Xers (just busting your chops, my gentle Gen X readers). Feedback and improvement are iterative processes. They can—and should—be repeated over and over. Workers can ask for feedback, devise an improvement plan, seek accountability from coworkers, and then check in again after a time—rinse and repeat. With enough support and work, greatness at work is achievable by all. As workers become engaged with the process and take stock of their improvements, they are likely to become motivated to continue.

Chapter 10: Teeming with Teams

"The strength of a team is each individual team member. The strength of each member is the team."

Phil Jackson

In large organizations, teams—not individuals—act as the basic human unit of production. Individuals and their roles comprise teams, but it is generally the team itself that executes business goals. The modern economy is complex and so are the businesses that contribute to it. A single person seldom functions independently within an organization. People function within the context of their teams.

In some instances, a small company may be a single team. More often, each department within a company will have a number of teams. Generally, in the modern economy, teams exist as fluid and overlapping groups of workers that are assigned to collaborate with different people in different ways. Large and efficient organizations retain fluid pools of workers that move in and out of various teams. Professor Amy C. Edmondson of Harvard Business School makes this point well in her 2014 book *Teaming*, in which she emphasizes that, while *team* is a noun, *teaming* is a verb. While we tend to conceive of teams as being a defined group of people, today's companies are often bringing different workers together to collaborate on various projects, often for only a limited time. Teams are constantly forming, evolving, and dissolving. The average corporate worker is collaborating with a number of teams at any given time. These teams are rarely permanent, especially in the context of project-based work. Given this level of fluidity, the practice of matching and handling teams becomes an ongoing process of critical importance.

While teams are the basic building blocks of organizations, individuals are the basic building blocks of teams. Teaming is the science of assembling those individuals into efficient teams. In order to do that effectively, team leaders and their managers need to create teams that are attentive to group dynamics. They must understand how individual team members work and communicate most effectively so that they can implement policies and systems that cater to individuals in service of the collective. This requires understanding the individuals on your team and determining how they fit into the context of the whole.

As was made clear at the outset of this book, individuals have many identities, experiences, histories, and other factors that shape who they are and how they move through the world. This book focuses on just one of those identities, generational cohorts, as that is our subject here—and it is a *big* one.

Generations group millions and millions of people together based on a variety of shared traits. The term "generational cohort" is shorthand for the many shared experiences and influences that shape people who were shaped by the same time and events. The broad nature of generational identity is why, in my opinion, managers should give it extra attention when assembling and managing teams. Our generational identities shape how we interact with others in powerful and multivariate ways. This is true for team members as well as team leaders, the latter of which must work hard to accommodate the former if they aspire to establish optimal team dynamics and performance.

The Boomer Handshake

Generational cohorts are a product of their times, particularly the times in which they were raised. Our formative years are when we learn to interact with other people, both from parents and friends; and the habits formed in childhood follow us through life. Interpersonal habits learned in childhood have a profound impact on how adults interact with others in a professional environment.

Boomers generally pride themselves on being able to read people. They're confident about their ability to understand others, which isn't surprising given that young boomers always seemed to be part of a group, be it with kids from the neighborhoods or classmates in crowded classrooms. They were likely to have a stay-at-home mother, as well as a number of siblings due to the rising fertility rates that caused the baby boom. When mom needed a break, she would tell the kids to "go outside and play." This was before the ensuing paranoia and fear around "stranger danger;" this was a simpler time when kids could roam safely and freely around the neighborhood. People often knew their neighbors. Most parents let their kids wander the neighborhood freely during the day, with other parents within earshot.

We boomers were always outside playing as kids. We didn't have social media or video games to keep us in the house. There was only so much an old pair of rabbit ears could get on the television, much of it geared toward adults. The house was often quite boring, so we were frequently outside playing with the other neighborhood kids. This was our first introduction to what you might call "networking," and it looked very much like networking in that we met in groups and talked face-to-face.

These early interactions influenced how boomers connect as adults. We prefer to meet up in person. We don't mind crowds or groups. We are the last of the ardent joiners. In *Bowling Alone*, political scientist Robert D. Putnam cataloged American's declining participation in social groups, particularly those that meet in person. The boomers are the last generation to do so in great numbers. Boomers join meetups, community boards, and social groups in a way that younger people rarely do these days. Younger generations simply don't engage in face-to-face social interactions in the same way. One reason is they have more alternatives to face-to-face meetings.

This tendency toward joining and face-to-face interaction affects how boomers behave on teams. We are a tactile bunch that prefers to hold meetings in person so that we can look you in the eyes and shake your hand. This is the way we can "size you up," a uniquely boomer phrase and concept. This is also how we establish trust and personal connections. This does *not* mean that boomers necessarily make unfounded assumptions based on stereotypes. We just need that face-to-face interaction to build trust and a connection. It is how boomers have traditionally gotten to know new people.

Another learned behavior boomers picked up in childhood is respect for, or at least deference to, authority. This, too, was formed at a young age. What our parents said went, no questions asked. The same was true at school, where the teacher was in charge, period, end of story. We didn't question, certainly not aloud, but often not even internally. As a child, we had to participate regularly in nuclear attack drills. I would dutifully crawl underneath my desk and put my hands over my head as if this would somehow magically save me from being vaporized in an atomic blast. It wasn't until years later that it occurred to me how compliant I had been.

This adherence to authority followed me into the workplace, where I understood that the boss was the boss and not to be second-guessed. When my bosses gave misguided or nonsensical orders, I would never balk (in his presence). Ill-conceived directives were still directives, and I was taught to follow them. As I have gotten older and become more discerning of the world around me, I still feel a twinge of panic or the pang of guilt when forced to defy or question authority.

The boomers' deference to authority, combined with our preference for in-person communication, shapes the way we approach teaming, especially when in positions of leadership. We tend to consider ourselves team players that shoot straight and get things done. "Shooting straight" often means "telling it like it is," which is a reflection of our hierarchical thinking. Telling it like it is implies that there is an objective reality, *our* reality. We aren't just saying this is how things *should* be, though we probably do think so, but rather that this is how things just *are*. We are the boss, what we say goes, and things get done our way. Boomers will delegate, but when they run teams there is almost always a clearly designated leader that gets the final say. They see this as the natural order and in no way unduly controlling. We were raised in the command-and-control economy—we see this mentality as *appropriately* controlling! After all, the team leader is responsible for the team outcome.

Ultimately, the buck stops with the person in charge, so it only makes sense for the person on top to call the shots. This attitude does not mean that boomers in leadership are particularly ruthless or unkind. Most boomers are, of course, kind, rational, and reasonable leaders. They genuinely *care* about the people on their teams. They see it as their duty to bring the team together, a noble goal.

Savvy leaders, even among us boomers, realize that allowing employees control over the decisions they make at work leads to higher engagement, more productive outcomes, and a greater sense of commitment. However, in times of stress, even the most experienced leaders can default to old habits. We go back to doing things "our way," even if we know we shouldn't.

Of course, "our way" mirrors our preferences. Boomers emphasize face-to-face interaction, as is our habit, when teaming. By way of example, boomers tend to be fond of launching new projects with the kickoff meeting. They may get everyone together first thing, face-to-face, to meet each other and talk about the project. In addition to setting the ground rules, they use this time to introduce everyone and get the team off on the right foot. As the project unfolds, these live meetings become part of the process. Frankly, any prudent team leader would have a kickoff meeting, it is just that boomers may not consider or think of alternatives to their preferred approach. Boomers value and recognize the importance of forging relationships. They will allocate more than sufficient time to share information, reminisce, or give inspirational talks whenever possible, which can make team meetings seem to drag on for their younger cohorts on the team.

Boomers don't see this as time wasted, though—it is time spent bringing the team together, which they see as their duty as leaders.

Based on their previous experiences and successes, they believe this style of working is best since it works best for them. They prioritize bringing the team together from the start. They will even encourage team members to socialize together on and off the clock.

While some may not like this approach, it can be effective. Spending time together does build camaraderie. What distinguishes boomers from other generations is that they are more apt to inspire by sharing "war stories" and their experiences related to being on similar teams. Their approach can differ from millennials, for instance, in that they are products of dialogues and as a consequence are not as prone to soliloquies. Boomers with leadership talent can and do inspire people and bring their teams together in this way. Their work style may not suit everyone, but it does get work done. Their idea of teamwork may be biased toward them telling the teams what to do and the team doing as it's told, but again, this gets results. The command-and-control model may not be the most democratic leadership paradigm, but it works.

But are there other approaches to getting similar results? We know that widespread worker disengagement, as was discussed earlier in this book, is the result of people being forced to work in environments and manners that don't suit their preferences and inclinations. We also know that keeping workers engaged improves productivity as well as worker satisfaction. Boomers, again, out of a habit that has served them so well, may be missing an opportunity here. While boomer managers may be getting results, they might consider alternatives as to how their individual workers would prefer to work rather than just assuming one size fits all.

This is a major issue for the generations that follow boomers, as they often have very different approaches to both work and teamwork. When boomers are in charge, their hierarchical nature often ignores or suppresses subordinates' preferences. While boomers are quick to bring people together to talk about the project and the team, what they often neglect to do is talk about *how* the team could be run or the work could be done. The typical boomer in leadership already knows those things, likely from their past experience, and they are quick to direct the actions of others, no questions asked. Well, maybe one question, "Is this clear?" which really wasn't meant as a question, per se, but rather as a statement in search of an affirmation.

Gen X Joins the Team

Gen X has a very different communication style that can be observed in how they choose to run teams. Unlike boomers, who are quick to arrange interactions in order to build relationships between all team members, Gen Xers generally see no need to force interactions. They aren't like boomers in this regard. They don't need to "size you up" in person. They don't need to spend time just rubbing elbows. They put the work first and allow relationships to build organically over time. This allows them to judge others on their actual performance, not subjective initial impressions, which, for some of them, is often little more than office politics. The way into Gen X's good graces is to prove you can do the work. You have to literally earn their trust by delivering successful outcomes.

To be clear, Gen Xers *do* form special working relationships. In fact, they often build very close relationships, but they do so over time—lots and lots of time. They are more selective, or possibly cautious, about whom they trust, but once you earn their trust, they are fiercely loyal.

Gen X's approach to relationships was also formed in childhood. Like boomers, Gen X latchkey kids were "free-rangers." However, they weren't on the streets with the neighborhood kids. They were hanging out at someone's house while their parents were away. This allowed them to forge intimate relationships with a few trusted friends. These relationships could last a lifetime. While all generations form long and enduring friendships, of course, this was the *primary* way that Gen X learned to socialize. Their lives are marked by these incredibly intimate relationships that were built slowly, over time.

As adults, I believe Gen Xers tend toward the same kind of relationships in both their professional and personal lives. Those in leadership tend to reuse the same people on their teams. They may be slow to accept new members on a team whose competency hasn't been established. They may be prone to question if a new person is really needed, especially if this new person will impact the existing team dynamics. However, once someone has proven their mettle, Gen Xers will rally behind and defend them. It's that same selective nature they developed as children carried over into adulthood.

Gen X managers are, on average, more hands-off than boomer managers. This isn't apathy, as Gen X is so often maligned, but a sign of respect and consideration. Gen Xers grew up figuring out things on their own. As teenagers, they often came home to empty houses with their parents away at work or possibly living separately. It was often up to the kids to make their own meals and get started on homework or chores unprompted. This made Gen X uniquely self-sufficient. They prefer to operate independently. They find micromanagement intrusive and often find team building exercises pointless.

When in management positions, Gen Xers often tend to

operate teams with loose structures that allow team members plenty of autonomy. Rather than adhere to a specific meeting schedule, they may have meetings only when it is necessary and probably elect to communicate electronically. They, like their team members, have lives outside of work, which in their case are a priority, and therefore, they are more willing to consider alternatives. They are more likely to adhere to meeting the objectives than to the process used in achieving them.

Since there is no single best way to run a team, it would be great if everyone shared their preferences and proclivities. Of course, this is not the case. Boomers generally value interaction as an inherent good that builds camaraderie. Millennials, who are collaborative and engaging by nature, may find their Gen X managers distant and unsupportive. New hires, in particular, may find Gen X's style of management unwelcoming. With time, and once a relationship is established, they may develop an appreciation for their Gen X managers, but getting there can be a long, arduous process. Millennials may be especially bothered by this arrangement at first, as they want guidance (which anyone new to a position will need) and thrive on open discussions. Their Gen X managers are likely to find these needs, well, *needy*.

This mismatch in interpersonal dynamics can cause frustration and hurt feelings. This is often the result of misinterpretation. People naturally assume intent based on what an action would mean if they themselves took it. Gen Xers only micromanage workers they either don't trust or those they are not confident have a reasonable level of competency. But boomers are more likely to appear to micromanage everyone by wanting frequent status report updates. This can lead Gen Xers to incorrectly believe that their boomer superiors do not trust them or their work. Likewise, Gen Xers are generally very independent. When millennials ask questions about something they could figure out on their own, Gen Xers may see this as a sign of incompetency, sloth, or neediness. In truth, millennials are just more collaborative by nature. They aren't necessarily asking questions because they *can't* make a decision on their own—they may be doing so because they *want* to make the decision with others.

This works in the other direction as well, of course. Boomers and millennials may find Gen Xers cold or aloof when they are merely giving people the space and autonomy that they themselves would want.

Using your own worldview and experience to gauge other people's intent is an assumptive leap. We must be mindful of our own biases and assumptions when trying to understand others. We should also be mindful of how we might be perceived by others. We have to work together here to understand and accommodate one another. Gen Xers should be aware that this style of management may make them appear as something other than they really are. Likewise, boomers, millennials, and Gen Zers should be careful about how they read highly independent and pragmatic workers, be they Gen Xers or not. *We would all benefit from more charitable readings of each other and a more accommodating nature.*

The Concordant, Collaborative, and Occasionally Cacophonous Millennials

While Gen X might have been able to keep a low profile and push through the boomer approach to teaming when necessary, the millennial generation has not found this to be as tolerable. The incongruence between their early life experiences and the modern workplace makes it impossible for them to keep quiet (as if that was ever a possibility) about how their teams are being run. Furthermore, while keeping quiet might be a strategy that worked for a disaffected Gen X, it does not conform to the millennials' nature. They were raised to be comfortable engaging with authority figures to discuss issues. Expecting them to accept the status quo and remain silent only makes them more frustrated.

Millennials were raised under what sociologist Annette Lareau, author of *Unequal Childhoods*, called "concerted cultivation," which is a style of parenting meant to foster a child's talents through active participation. This kind of parenting gave millennials their Engage-Discuss mindset. Their parents encouraged them to be highly participatory. They were taught to ask questions and expected to engage in dialogue, a habit they carried into adulthood. They expect team leaders to include them in open discussion and decision-making just as their parents included them in decisions about vacations or relocation. If they were going to have to spend two weeks somewhere or switch school districts, millennial children expected a say in the matter. Their parents raised them to believe that participation meant each and every family member got a vote. In school, they learned to collaborate on group projects and participated in peer study groups. These groups were nonhierarchical and, since they were simply classmates, collaboration and collective participation were encouraged.

Now that millennials are in the workplace and on teams, they still expect a seat at the table and a say in how things are run. Unfortunately, these expectations may put them at odds with hierarchical boomer managers and independent-minded Gen X team leaders, especially for young millennials who haven't yet risen through the ranks or proven themselves. Millennials expect to be fully included right from the get-go, which can offend boomers who might misinterpret assertiveness and engagement as insubordination or disrespect. Gen X managers may find millennials arrogant for expecting a starring role before having proven their own competency. These assumptions, usually untrue and based on misunderstandings, do not take into account how incongruent most workplace teams are with how millennials were raised to interact with authority figures. It's not that millennials aren't good at collaborating or being team players—it's that they are often seen as *too* collaborative for certain leaders' expectations of them relative to what they, the boomer or Gen X leaders, were like at that age.

The incongruence that millennials feel in the workplace extends beyond team dynamics to most workplace communications, potentially leaving them feeling alienated at work. Millennials struggle to feel connected to others in environments that don't cater—and are often openly hostile—to their sensibilities. Boomers forge connections almost by default, through an inherent sense of team identity. Gen Xers form connections slowly, but surely, as they work with people. But millennials often need to engage in discussion to build connections. They build connections by sharing things about themselves and learning from others.

This, too, can be traced back to their early lives. Their parents always took an explicit interest in what their children felt and thought. Millennials were encouraged to think about who they were as individuals and share this with others. This impulse has been reinforced by participation in social media. Many millennials, and to some extent, albeit selectively, Gen Zers as well, grew up broadcasting their thoughts and interests to the world. Though often thought of as narcissistic and self-absorbed, most millennials actually take a deep interest in other people. They don't just post to Facebook and Instagram—most of the time spent on these sites involves scrolling through other people's profiles and posts. Building connections by sharing experiences and viewpoints requires mindful, active *listening*, not just broadcasting, and millennials do both. Their way of connecting with and showing interest in others is different from those who came before, but it is no less genuine and heartfelt. I should also note that Gen Zers, having seen the mistakes millennials made early on in sharing with the world who they are on a medium seen by all, are themselves more selective. While also users of social media, they are more discriminatory in what they say and to whom they say it. They have curated selves that may vary depending upon who they want to be seen as.

Of course, this is not how their more senior cohorts tend to see such sharing by millennials or Gen Zers. Gen Xers are prone to see this sharing as *over*sharing. Boomers are likely to find it simply inappropriate. They can see this sharing as overly performative and self-promoting. It is the equivalent of a real-life verbal selfie. They don't always understand that this is a genuine attempt to build connections. Millennials (and Gen Zers) grew up differently and have different ways of behaving and being. However, workers from a different generation often fail to appreciate what motivates their behavior, which we interpret under our own quite different generational perspective. This leads to angry screeds that begin, "When I was your age . . ." But this ultimately misses the point and applies the boomer's motivation to the millennial's behavior when, in fact, the millennial had an entirely different motivation.

Being so misinterpreted has been an unfortunate hallmark of the millennial experience. Their assertiveness has often been interpreted (or misinterpreted) as arrogance, their participatory nature and enthusiasm as poor form, their inquisitiveness as unprofessional and lacking in respect. Typical observations: "They are needy." "They talk too much." "They ask too many questions." "They won't just do what they are told." "They don't know they're not in charge."

While millennials get maligned for these behaviors, the truth is that they make for highly collaborative team players who aren't afraid to speak up or participate. They may not thrive in hierarchical or atomized teams, but they do work well with others. Collaboration is in their generational veins. They are great team players—they were literally raised to work together. If more organizations and managers would simply embrace these qualities in millennials, rather than castigating them for what we think it says about them, we could build teams that suit younger workers and also function better. Being collaborative and assertive are *positive* traits. Managers should be happy to have enthusiastic workers that want to get involved. If more senior managers weren't so quick to assign malintent to these habits, they might see just how much millennials have to offer. Millennials might even serve as the model for a better, more democratic workplace—the very kind that their boomer and Gen X parents raised them to expect.

If we want to reduce these misjudgments and leverage the millennial's collaborative nature for collective advantage, leadership will have to be more accommodating. Boomers will have to be less hierarchical and Gen X less independent and more interdependent. As new workers come into the workplace, the old guard must make space for other ways of doing things. They must democratize the workplace enough so that every new generation feels that they have a voice, which is really all millennial workers are expecting. We will also soon have to make room for Gen Zers as well, who will be equally vocal in broadcasting their wants and desires.

This is not to suggest that teams should not have designated leaders. Of course, they should. Someone has to manage the team and assume ultimate and ongoing responsibility. However, in a collaborative model of teaming that would better suit millennial sensibilities, the team leader is there to lead, not in a command-and-control manner but rather in a manner that is facilitative or directive depending on what is appropriate to the needs of the team at the time. The team leader becomes coach and referee. Sure, they can still call the shots, and sometimes have to, but they will generally get better results from taking the team's preferences and needs into account. Everyone's thoughts and opinions get heard and considered, though not necessarily implemented, and everyone ultimately understands the "why" behind a decision. We may not all agree, but we all understand the reasoning, and we all consent to a shared set of rules. This consent and consensus require that everyone on the team understands why things are done the way they are and feel included in the decision-making process.

Managing the Pushback

Of course, adapting to new ways of doing things is rarely painless. As a boomer, I sometimes find it challenging to work with millennials. It can feel like they are trying to take over the team.

A law firm once invited me to speak on a panel about generational differences with a millennial, a Gen Xer, and another boomer. I was to be both a participant and the moderator. Everyone else on the panel was a lawyer. I had been invited because of my expertise in generational theory. They were there to offer their personal perspectives while I would facilitate and lead the discussion.

We had a series of conference calls beforehand to discuss how we would run the panel and what we would discuss. Despite my role as the facilitator and the only one with a background in generational differences, I was not given the deference I expected. The millennial speaker immediately started issuing off-the-cuff suggestions about how to run the panel and what we should cover. I was put off that she seemed to think she was running the show when—*ahem*—certain *other* people on the line had far more expertise on the topic at hand. Only *one* of us had spent years reviewing relevant research . . . and it wasn't her. Nonetheless, she had no reservations about issuing her opinions first. Never mind that I had the expertise, never mind that I was the moderator, never mind that I was thirty years her senior.

While it was an unrelated conflict of interest that later forced me to withdraw from the panel, I was relieved to be free from the ideas and suggestions posed by this vocal and assertive young person. I felt, at the time, disrespected. I had been invited by the organization to be the facilitator, not her. I was the one with the expertise. And, if I'm being honest, it offended me that a person so much younger would talk over someone thirty years her senior. But more important than just being deferential to my age, it was my view that the person responsible for the panel discussion and gifted with the relevant expertise should be calling the shots— all very boomer positions to take. It annoyed me that this person who was significantly younger and had significantly less knowledge on the topic had tried to take over.

In the years since, I have come to accept my misinterpretation of the situation. Although, truth be told, thinking back on the exchange still irks me. Armed with hindsight 20/20, I know that this was about my boomer biases and misinterpretation of her intentions. Her behavior certainly *felt* inappropriate at the time, but again, with the benefit of hindsight, one could argue that it wasn't rudeness but simply my discomfort with her method of participation, but it still doesn't make her, in my mind, less rude. Maybe she was out of line, maybe not. It doesn't matter now. There are two takeaways here.

First, our perception is not necessarily indicative of what is actually happening. Perception is subjective. My reality was not her reality. While my feelings were valid and worthy of consideration, my assumption about her intent was off base. Millennials aren't necessarily trying to take over the team when they behave assertively. This is simply how many of them engage and communicate. They are accustomed to helping chart the course when aboard the ship. We need not assume that all voices from the deck are plotting to take over the helm. Her input may have been merely participatory, not mutinous, and looking at these situations through the lens of generational differences reveals that we often completely misinterpret one another.

Second, we are all human and fallible. The entire point of this book is to improve our understanding of each other and embrace our differences so that the workplace will be better for all. But stating that intention and living it as a reality are two different things. Saying it is easy. *Doing* it can be difficult. But we must try. We must try until it becomes our habit. We are deeply attached to our old habits and overcoming them takes work.

This kind of reflection isn't easy, neither is deference and accommodation. You have to work against your own biases and be willing to make sacrifices toward mutual accommodation. So will the people you are working with. But the truth is that many people have been making these sacrifices, just less equitably, all along. Remember, Gen Xers have been keeping their heads down to accommodate boomers for years. Millennials are often routinely working on teams that fail to accommodate their differences. Compromise should be equitable—that's the whole point of a compromise—and we won't achieve real equity unless we all actively listen to each other.

People in leadership positions who are significantly older than their reports typically have more experience and expertise (or they should, at any rate). It is not a fault of the young that they are less experienced. They simply haven't been at work as long. Having to pause and take input from them can feel like a waste of time and even maddening when under pressure. In tough situations, when a deadline looms, the last thing I want to do is pause and explain myself to a subordinate and negotiate basic processes and policies. As a boomer steeped in a long tradition of deference to authority, I sometimes just want them to do as they're told. But toiling to make them simply do as they are told would only end in a Pyrrhic victory at best. I could get their compliance, but I would never get their commitment.

Of course, that's not how they see things. They are simply playing by a different set of rules. The younger generations see collaboration and discussion as the way to get things done quickly. They may be puzzled and frustrated that I won't just sit down and talk with them so they can get back to work. This makes total sense if you accept that, from their view, it is *me* that is impeding the process. They have a collaborative worldview in which all team members are respected and given a voice. In their view, it is me that is the problem. Sometimes, I have come to begrudgingly admit, they are not wrong.

In order to get along, we must all recognize our own biases *as biases*. Doing so prevents you from automatically interpreting differences as deficiencies. Compromise and deference will never make sense, especially to team leaders, until you can see things from the other perspective. In fact, managers that think they are right *shouldn't* compromise. But you better make sure you are actually right and not just biased. And, if you are right, you better take the time to explain why you are right if you seek commitment from team members regardless of their generational cohort.

Team leaders should be allowed to lean toward their own preferences. It is within their rights to make decisions against the team's wishes. You don't have to be a boomer or authoritarian to believe that team leaders ultimately own the decision. Team leaders should be free to manage their teams in the way they deem most appropriate. However, prudent managers consider their reports' wants and preferences. When those preferences don't impede the larger goal, there is no good reason not to accommodate them. Doing so can keep workers more engaged and thus productive.

Sometimes, managers cannot and should not cater to what the team wants. What we *want* isn't always what we *need*. An experienced boomer leading a team of very young millennials or Gen Z graduates may *need* to implement a hierarchical structure with such green recruits. This isn't necessarily about the manager's generational bias so much as what the team needs. On the other hand, a team of slightly older millennials with a few years of experience under their belts might benefit from being run more democratically since they have the knowledge and experience to govern themselves. Regardless of the generational cohort, the secret to managing is to match your behavior to the needs of the team and team members.

Setting the Rules of the Game—Together

So how do we resolve tensions between disgruntled team members and the harassed managers that often find their young team members recalcitrant? The first step is to realize that both are dissatisfied for the same reasons. They don't understand where the opposing viewpoint is coming from. They may not even recognize it as an opposing viewpoint. Younger managers do not understand why their bosses won't listen. Older managers are asking the same thing—why won't they *listen*?

The answer: each side is operating by a different set of rules grounded in different assumptions and worldviews. They don't necessarily have to adopt each other's perspectives, and the people on top get the final say, but everyone should try to understand one another. *Understanding is a prerequisite to finding a workable compromise.*

Second, teams need to adopt a set of rules upon which everyone can agree. Whatever approach a team takes, everyone has to understand the rules. This is critical to avoiding misunderstandings and misinterpretations. There are lots of viable ways to run teams, but everyone needs to land in the same place. Everyone has to know and accept the expressed rules.

Transparency is critical here. The formal rules are often only the tip of the iceberg when it comes to how teams operate. Norms and unwritten assumptions often govern how teams operate just as much, if not more, than the formal rules. These norms are understandings about what the rules mean. Managers often assume that these norms are clear when they are not. People may not even find out about these informal rules until they are reprimanded for violating them. Worse still, the violator may not be made aware of the violation, instead, they become the subject of scorn and hidden discussion. Managers will sometimes talk with other managers about employees that break these unspoken rules without even thinking of raising the issue with the employee. "They should just *know* not to do that," they might say, as if the employee should have learned something by osmosis without ever being told. Think back to the beginning of the book and the situation with Bob's negative reaction to Zach and Becca's behavior at the meeting. Had Bob filled them in on their roles before the meeting and his expectations of when and where it would be appropriate for them to participate given the audience, everyone on the team would have experienced a different and better outcome.

Violating these unspoken rules can lead them down the path to termination or a growing level of frustration that ultimately results in them quitting. Avoid such confusion and miscommunication by making the implicit explicit. Do away with the assumption that the informal rules are known and understood by all by discussing them openly. Doing so allows team leaders to have actual open discussions about policy and expectations.

Finally, make sure that the discussions are open, engaging, and inclusive. The rules should be crafted to accommodate everyone as much as possible, whenever possible. Managers often adopt policies and protocols that suit how they do business. This forces teams to conform to the preferences of team leaders even when there is no benefit to doing so. In fact, there is always a cost to making people work in ways that don't suit them. Giving team members clear expectations of the specific role they are assigned will foster commitment. Had Becca been told in advance that she would be responsible for presenting some crucial information if the questions pertinent to it were brought up in the meeting then she would have been excited and prepared to answer them. Conversely, younger colleagues will be less engaged and more frustrated by their work and work interactions if they are forced to guess, and worse still, if guessing wrong leads to a reprimand. Managers themselves would be better served by embracing differences and working to accommodate everyone as much as possible.

Consider this the "maximum engagement" approach to teaming. How can the team function in a way that will make everyone feel as engaged as possible? Obviously, when multiple parties collaborate, everyone will need to acknowledge and accept that a team cannot necessarily accommodate everyone's preferences. But by negotiating processes, which is really all millennials are asking for, we can create an environment where everyone feels seen and heard. This will make millennials and Gen Zers happier and boomers less frustrated, and it will enhance the overall feelings of engagement and inclusion. Even those Gen Xers who would rather just "go with the flow" will benefit from flexible systems that accommodate that desire. This may seem like it is merely catering to millennials, but that is only because their approach to teaming is of open discussion and collaboration. We must keep this in mind. When we cater to these preferences, we also cater to those who have other needs and demands, whatever they may be.

Gen Zers, having entered the workplace, are also expecting both a clear indication of why things are done a certain way and a say in how they should be done. They are not, however, simply another crop of millennials. Having grown up under different circumstances, they will have their own set of teaming "quirks" that will likely begin to incite criticism as more of them make their way into the workplace.

Remember, while a generational lens can be helpful, it is not the only factor influencing an individual's preferences. Team members have a number of other identities, including gender, racial, cognitive, and cultural differences that can influence their preferences. As I have said previously, the primary goal of this book is to examine generational differences, these other identities and factors can be just as (or perhaps even more) relevant in determining a person's overall preferences. A generational lens can provide insight and context into a person but should not be used to stereotype individuals. When in doubt, take a page from the millennials and just ask people what they prefer. Ask . . . and then *listen*.

They may not even always know what they want. Sometimes, you have to help them figure it out. You may need to work with your team to surface their hidden preferences. One way of doing this is with communication preference instruments, under vendor names such as the DISC or Insights. These and other similar instruments are simple tools that can help surface differences in communication styles and provide a mechanism for accommodating those differences. Work with team members to discover how they work best.

This is where being a good facilitator and guide is key. Decide what rules work best for you as the team leader. Get your team's input and establish their preferences. Then let the negotiations begin. Discussions should be open and transparent as you work toward a set of rules that work best for everyone. Concede where it makes sense. Compromise when possible. Draw the line as necessary, but always explain your reasoning thoroughly.

Your team will thank you for it—someday. And if not, you can always take solace in the fact that these young millennials will someday have to form their own teams, indeed many of them already are. These teams will include young Gen Z workers, and they will have their own sets of preferences. They will have their own habits and work styles, and while we don't yet know how these will manifest in the workplace, we can be sure that they will. Having learned, from you, their manager, on how to listen and work through challenges together, you will have acted as a role model and help set the next generation up to succeed.

Chapter 11: "Things a Mentor Would Do!"

"We need to remember across generations that there is as much to learn as there is to teach."

Gloria Steinem

Dick Clark was an entertainment icon best known for his decades-long run as the television host of *American Bandstand* and the annual *New Year's Rockin' Eve* broadcasts from Times Square. Mr. Clark was also the host of the gameshow *The $10,000 Pyramid* when it debuted in 1973. I loved *The $10,000 Pyramid*. The format was simple: two competing teams, each pairing a contestant with a celebrity—the Brad Pitt or Taylor Swift of the day. One of the pair gave clues—naming things that belonged to a category—while the other player attempted to guess the category. Speed was key: rounds were timed and as soon as *the guesser* correctly named the category (often with tremendous gusto and volume) *the clue-giver* moved to the next section of the pyramid, with the team accumulating prize money along the way. It was good, clean, heart-pounding fun. Let's play. Here are your clues: "share wisdom, teach, serve as a guide, give advice, provide coaching, act as a sounding board, explain unwritten rules, lend support and encouragement . . ." And you respond: "Things a mentor would do!" Ding—we have a winner!

A mentor shares his or her experience, wisdom, and knowledge with someone who has not accumulated those things to the same degree. Mentors are helpful guides to navigating the many barriers and enablers in the workplace. With earned trust and shared personal experience these relationships can grow to last a lifetime, continuing even when mentor and mentee no longer work for the same organization. This helps explain why so many organizations have instituted formal mentoring programs: they can be deeply rewarding for the participants and elevate both individual and company performance. Unfortunately, many of these well-intentioned mentoring programs used forced pairings in an attempt to replicate what can be best described as organic success stories. Another challenge to the success of formal mentoring programs is their failure to acknowledge the generational dynamics frequently at play. That is where we will focus our attention. But first, back in the time machine for a quick story . . .

My first *professional* mentor, if we define the concept loosely enough to include primary school, was my Hickory Township Middle School shop teacher, Woodrow Davenport. (We called him Mr. Davenport to his face and Woody behind his back because being a Woody is funny to a twelve-year-old.) Of course, my parents had served as role models and mentors, but they were my parents. My shop teacher, Mr. Davenport, despite not being of blood relation, elected to invest extra time in my development. This wasn't part of his job description. He was paid to teach shop, not to inspire us. But he went above and beyond by allowing us to stay after school to work on our projects. He would walk around the class and give those of us who showed an interest in shop some extra tips, guidance, and advice. No one was forcing him to do these things. He was more than just a teacher. He was, in retrospect, a mentor.

So strong was his impression on me that my few memories of middle school are from his shop class. The big dusty room. The smell of sawdust and charred wood. Squinting through the scratches in my plastic safety goggles. Pulling splinters out of my fingers. This is what I remember of middle school; this and little else.

It goes without saying that during the late sixties shop class was a decidedly masculine environment. Boys took shop while girls took home economics, a function of the binary gender roles of the time. Girls were expected to become wives that would see after the household. Boys were expected to learn "practical" things, which apparently included building an ornate wooden table lamp in the form of a rearing stallion. While I won't speak for others, learning to use a lathe hasn't been relevant to my own career. It was my first and last experience using heavy machinery—unless you count the industrial dishwasher I got to know well while working as a busboy one summer at the Oak Room, Hickory's swankiest restaurant. Nonetheless, shop class meant something to me as a young boy.

My experience in shop class gave me time with a male role model other than my father. This was a positive experience. At only four foot nine inches tall, I wasn't exactly athlete material and never had a coach take an interest in me. So, it was probably good to have a positive male role model in the shop teacher—and how very stereotypically male Woody Davenport was, I might add.

It was as if the school had recruited Mr. Davenport from Central Casting (an actual place) to play the part of a shop teacher. His voice was raspy and gruff. He was grandfatherly in both look and demeanor. I will never forget the scars and nicks on his fingers from close calls with table saws and slips of the hammer. This was probably why he was such a stickler for safety. Lucky for me, as I still have all ten digits. He taught us to respect the machines. They were dangerous but useful, and he loved what one could do with them. It was a love and a passion he shared with us, particularly those of us who showed interest in tapping his wealth of experience.

I was one of those individuals. I found Mr. Davenport and the shop experience immensely satisfying—not only for what we were learning but for how we were being taught. It was the first and only time I crafted something of note with my hands. My journey over the course of that school year—from clumsy and dubious to reasonably capable and markedly more confident—was profound. Mr. Davenport was patient when we made mistakes, and he made it a point to recognize our progress. Mr. Davenport was "catching us doing something right" long before that phrase became part of the enlightened manager's lexicon. This motivated me to work hard to get better. By the end of the year, I had crafted and painted my first (and only) galloping horse lamp. Flicking the tail turned on the bulb, a work of true genius, if I do say so myself. No matter that everyone in the class had made the exact same lamp, I was immensely proud of mine. I had built it from scratch, cutting the wood, assembling the lamp, wiring the parts, and carefully painting it. I had done it myself, but not alone. Mr. Davenport was there to guide me the whole way. He kept us engaged and let us fail upward until finally, we had the painted pine stallion lamps of our dreams.

While our official student-teacher relationship ended after he handed out final grades, my view of Mr. Davenport was fundamentally changed. We acknowledged each other when we passed in the halls—stopping for a brief chat a time or two but more often exchanging a nod and a smile without breaking stride. I never had the need to seek Mr. Davenport's advice on miter saws or the intricacies of dovetail joinery, but it mattered knowing I could approach him about those topics or whatever else was on my young mind.

I was so inspired by my shop experience that I briefly considered a career in architecture. For his part, I suspect Mr. Davenport appreciated his role in our relationship too. We were making lamps. He was making *us*. His mentorship shaped many of us as young people. What more rewarding thing is there to craft than a real live human being? His role in our creations is undeniable. Those piles of wood in the back of the room would never have become working lamps without him imparting his knowledge and us showing genuine interest in absorbing it. I shudder to think of the hideous fire hazard I would have created on my own. As an aside, I no longer have the lamp. Once I went off to college, it seemed to have mysteriously disappeared from my bedroom. I suspect my mother might have not found it as aesthetically pleasing as I thought it to be at the age of twelve.

Of course, we never thanked him; children are not exactly known for their consideration. But our lack of appreciation in no way diminished his role. The cycle of generations was playing out between us. The young are hungry for knowledge. Those who have lived and learned can find satisfaction in passing on a lifetime of lessons. He was mentoring me and my classmates. Later, we would continue the cycle and go on to mentor others.

The passing of the baton from one generation to the next is

the story of human history. We are social animals and mentorship is part of our long-term survival, central to our DNA. The ability to pass knowledge and culture down through the generations is a core feature of the human species. Generational turnover allows for cultural evolution to occur alongside biological evolution. Seen this way, mentoring contributes to generational change by passing wisdom down through the ages. It is a key part of what it means to be human.

Mentorship contributes to cultural evolution. The knowledge that is passed down to the next generation gets reinterpreted in a new context. Mentees learn from the mistakes of those who came before and reinterpret what they have been taught so that it can be applied to present circumstances.

No matter the size of their contribution, our mentors are all owed a debt of great gratitude. Unless you grew up alone in the woods, your achievements are not entirely your own. None of us are self-made; not really. We all stand on the shoulders of those who came before. We should be proud of our accomplishments. But our own raw effort is only part of the equation. We may run the race, but these people paved the way to the starting line.

These enabling advocates go by many names—parents, teachers, mentors, advisors, role models—but what they have in common is their impact: the positive contributions to our lives and careers. It's no wonder so many companies have instituted formal mentoring programs. The benefits to the employee (and by extension, to the business) can be profound. While mentoring produces good outcomes, formalizing the mentoring process presents problems and challenges.

The Potential Pitfalls of Institutionalized Mentorship

Mentorship is not new. It has been with us for all of human history. What has changed in recent times is mentorship *in the workplace*. Traditionally, professional mentor relationships arose organically. Mentors would discover some young person with potential and take them under their wing. This was an elective process. The mentor often saw their younger self reflected back at them in the protégé. Nothing about this was orchestrated. The mentor *wanted* to be a mentor. They would take time out of their day to cultivate and groom the young person to become something more. They offered advice and guidance freely. Though the mentor often occupied a superior position, the mentorship process was largely informal.

These emerging relationships were invaluable. If mentors have both experience and institutional knowledge, then workers with mentors are likely to perform better in their jobs and careers than those without mentors. This had led companies to match young workers with mentors which, on paper, makes complete sense. If mentorship improves performance, why not find everyone in the company a mentor? Don't have a mentor? We'll assign you one! Mentors for all! It's a nice thought but contrived and wholly unrealistic.

Mentorships are personal and intimate relationships. Before the rise of formal mentoring programs, no one planned to have a mentor. You were not asked who your mentor is *going* to be. But you were asked who your mentors *were*. We get asked if we *had* a mentor. These questions are always posed in the past tense for a reason: mentors are minted through the act of mentoring.

Mentorship is not something you can easily orchestrate. They are relationships that form only *after* establishing that mutual trust, intimacy, and respect. Mentoring relationships are a consequence of knowing and appreciating each other. Mentors take on mentees because they believe in them. The mentee enters the relationship because they respect the mentor and want to learn from them. While you can readily assign two people to each other, unless and until both parties feel they are benefiting from this assignment, it is a mentoring relationship in name only. This presumption that an assigned match will lead to a trusting and meaningful relationship is what concerns me.

True mentorship relations are between mentors that want to give advice and mentees that want to receive it. The mentor *wants* to be a mentor. The mentee wants guidance. When either one of these things is untrue, the program doesn't live up to its name. Both parties just go through the motions required of them. This can make both parties unhappy. The essence of the problem isn't with a program that matches junior people in need of experience with senior people who have it. The problem is with the presumptive nomenclature, the use of the word *mentoring*. Words have power and because of that maybe this isn't the right name for what companies are trying to create.

More and more companies are creating *mentoring programs*. They have become exceedingly common in the last few decades. This raises the question. Why are they suddenly so popular now? The value of mentorship is not new. We have known about it for many generations. Why are company leaders and managers only recently so keen on institutionalizing the creation of mentoring relationships?

In a word: millennials.

Guidance through the Generations

The institutionalization of mentorship is a formal response to millennials' desire for someone at work to take a deep and personal interest in their development. This has been documented in the Gallup Q12 employee engagement survey[20]. The Q12 survey helps organizations create a baseline for workplace engagement. One question in the survey asks respondents: *"Is there someone at work who encourages your development?"* Companies that do well on the survey have a favorable standing as a good place to work and that would mean they have a preponderance of yes responses to the question. Millennials want guidance. They were raised by parents and taught by teachers that engaged them directly from a young age. They became accustomed to working with authority figures that served as guides. In the workplace, millennials found the lack of built-in guides incongruent with their baseline expectations.

Millennials have a strong propensity to make their desires known and have been asking for someone to shepherd them through their careers. The solution was to create formal mentoring programs to address this need. Companies have been implementing these programs in various forms for a number of years. Millennials want advice, mentors give advice—ergo get me a mentor so I can get advice. Seems like a reasonable request. But the assignment, the creation of the pairing, is only the first step, the difficult part is creating and sustaining the trust-based relationship.

Young boomers, coming of age at a different time were

---

20 Marcus Buckingham and Curt Coffman, *First Break All the Rules*, (New York: Simon & Schuster, 1999), 28

certainly not asking for mentorship programs. They were quite happy to find mentors the old-fashioned way. In fact, they were utterly thrilled to do so. Boomers grew up with authority figures issuing them orders. If you will recall from previous chapters, Boomers were brought up under a Tell-Do paradigm in which their parents and teachers told them what to do and they did it. They may have come from loving families, but their parents and teachers didn't necessarily engage them in dialogues about their hopes and dreams. For many boomers, the person who became their mentor was quite possibly one of the first people to take an interest in them as a young professional.

This was quite a nice experience for a young boomer, made more so because it was so often incongruent with our upbringing. It was a pleasant surprise. We certainly weren't complaining when someone at work took an interest in our careers. Everyone wants people to take a genuine interest in them. Boomers that found such a person felt lucky. Any supervisor (or more experienced colleague) that would take someone under his or her wing and help them grow was truly special.

Given the social customs of the baby-boom era, these organic mentorship relationships were usually between younger and older men. Men held most of the positions of power, and they generally groomed other men for bigger and better things. There were, of course, women mentoring other women, but the men dominated the upper echelons of organizations. The character Peggy Olson as portrayed by Elizabeth Moss on the AMC show *Mad Men*, personifies this struggle that ambitious female baby boomers in the corporate world faced. Kudos to the women that were able to make this work, but it was indeed rare at the time. Thankfully, things have changed for women in society and the workplace. There are a growing number of cracks in the "glass ceiling," and we have just recently seen the first woman elected Vice President of the United States. There is more work to do in bringing full gender equality to the workplace but recent progress is encouraging.

Many boomers look back fondly on, and with great respect for, their early mentors. These young protégés invested time into learning from their mentors and took their advice seriously. They listened attentively. They emulated their practices. Those of us lucky enough to have a mentor felt grateful. We were fully aware that our mentors had chosen us just as much as we had chosen them. We wanted to impress them. We didn't want to let them down. We made sacrifices to impress them, which, in the days of the company man, meant making sacrifices to the company. Our mentors gave their all to the company. We did the same. This was how they noticed us in the first place.

Nothing about these relationships was forced. They were organic. They were professional, of course, but not professionalized. There were no policies in place. There weren't *mentorship programs*. There were no *"How to Be a Better Mentor in Five Easy Steps"* training courses. The relationship evolved. Our bosses selected us based on their gut feelings. Moving up the ranks required a senior executive willing to take you under his or her wing. It wasn't always fair, some people worthy of being mentored weren't, and others who might have wanted to be a mentor may not have been given the opportunity. It was a voluntary arrangement agreed upon by both parties.

As with other business practices inherited from the boomers, Generation X made little alteration to this organic model of mentorship. Gen Xers, more protective of their private lives than the boomers, were likely to be slower and more hesitant to enter into a deeply personal, often vulnerable, work relationship with their bosses. Boomers saw an authority figure who was actually interested in them as both a professional and a person, Gen Xers had a different view. Having learned to be self-sufficient at a young age, Gen Xers may not have wanted a *mentor*, but rather a *sponsor*. The distinction between a mentor and a sponsor is nuanced but important.

A mentor is interested in you and your career, a sponsor is interested in your career and is willing to intervene on your behalf in ways that could impact their own careers. While mentoring tends to be a supportive activity tied to listening and suggesting, sponsorship is proactive with the sponsor directing and strategizing. Figuring things out on their own, Gen X may have found being mentored somewhat limited. They didn't necessarily want to share their hopes and dreams, their dreams were private. The concept of a sponsor relationship that was all about advancing your career with the sponsor's direct help could have been more appealing. If companies had been more savvy, they would have offered *sponsorship programs* to young Gen Xers in the 1980s and '90s.

Gen X, as I have previously suggested, is suspicious of authority and that suspicion extends to the company man. When Gen X arrived at the workplace there was no drive to create mentoring programs in the same way that companies have done for millennials. Why? In my view, they grew up believing in meritocracy—if you put in the work, the work should speak for itself. Their parents raised them to come home and get things done. Their parents didn't care how it got done so long as it got done. This instilled Gen Xers with a pragmatic outlook. They didn't want to stay late in the office schmoozing and playing politics in the hope that some higher-up would take them under their wing. They had no interest in trying to be noticed. Their meritocratic viewpoint is noble, but—dare I say, as a boomer—a little utopian.

Mentors help a mentee "in seeing the forest for the trees." Another person's perspective, wisdom, and advice augment and help direct the meritorious.

Many Gen Xers didn't have time to go looking for mentors. If someone did come along and discover them, great, but otherwise, Gen X was busy. Mentorship—from the standpoint of the mentor and the mentee—takes effort. Mentors can offer advice, but the mentee has to listen and absorb that advice. You have to put that advice into practice. You have to report back and discuss your progress. When someone invests in you, they expect you to put in the effort to succeed. Despite being stereotyped as slackers, Gen Xers wanted to succeed as much as anyone else. They just wanted to do so on their terms and lacked the time for the boomer vision of mentorship. (As I mentioned, had these programs been modified and rebranded under the heading of *sponsorship*, then the explicit nature of the arrangement would have better aligned with Gen X sensibilities.)

Gen X is an interesting cohort. They might have been struggling to run a household with both parents working. They might have been a single parent. They were likely already putting lots of hours in at their jobs in addition to any other responsibilities. Gen X often found itself working more than those who came before due to changes in the economy, labor markets, and/or to being "sandwiched" by having responsibilities that may include both raising their children and caring for aging parents. For these and other reasons, Gen X did not prioritize finding mentors. Still, they did have to navigate the world the boomers created. Gen Xers may be slow to give their trust, but once they do, they can be, as I have already stated, fiercely loyal. So, while Gen Xers may not have been looking for mentors, they made surprisingly good mentees once a relationship was established.

Gen X, regardless of the extent of their self-sufficiency, still wants the support and affirmation of others. Companies realistically can only set up the situation. They can create the conditions by which a mentoring relationship can bloom, but they can't mandate it into existence. So, Gen X didn't typically ask for mentor programs. Like the boomers, they found their mentors organically, if they found them at all. Millennials, who actually do want someone to offer support and show interest in them at work, are different in that they are willing to speak up and make their desires known.

Millennials also aren't afraid of letting other people know whether or not their employer delivered the goods. Word travels fast in the modern world. People talk about their employers. They even post online about it. There are several Yelp-like review sites devoted to offering insights and information on an employer such as Glassdoor or The Vault, whether it is a massive international corporation valued at billions of dollars or a small local startup with a dozen employees. These reviews are a click away and they stay online forever.

Companies that depend on millennials with in-demand, portable skill sets cannot afford to be known as toxic or unsupportive workplaces. As we have established, Millennials are now the largest segment of the workforce and the primary source of trained young talent. They are the lifeblood of the workforce. Companies that lose access to this wellspring of talent risk becoming uncompetitive. In competitive industries, such as tech, recruitment of top talent is everything. Workers in these industries understand the value of their skill sets. They will go where they get the best offer—and the best offer is not reducible to only pay and benefits. Millennials want supportive workplace environments. Getting branded as a company that doesn't meet employee needs can be a liability or even a death knell for companies that must recruit top talent.

This can happen fast. Just consider the reputation of Facebook. One of the "Big Four" of big tech and an employer of the highest prestige, it has seen its reputation tarnished in recent years. Numerous media outlets reported on Facebook employees suddenly ashamed to admit that they work there after several high-profile scandals broke over the last few years. Facebook is obviously far from being a failure, but the change in workforce sentiment could seriously hamper their ability to attract and retain the absolute best talent. In a transactional labor market, where workers can take their skills elsewhere, employers *must* be attentive to young millennial and soon Gen Z workers' wants and needs in a way that they did not have to be with Gen X. This means paying close attention to what your employees are saying about your firm. It also means listening when your employees say they want mentors or anything else.

Regardless of generational cohort, at some time or another everyone wants or would benefit from the relationship with a mentor. The generational differences are more obvious in a particular group's willingness to lobby their employer to foster these relationships. Boomers were always grateful for their mentors. They simply didn't think about being demonstrative that prospective employers have them. They waited to be discovered by a higher-up that would take them under their wing. They waited patiently for this to happen as they would never deign to ask for such a thing. Gen Xers would not raise a hand and ask for mentors either. Their circumstances—entering the workplace in smaller numbers, during unstable economic times, without the benefit of Internet-enabled access to the inner workings of companies—did not prompt Gen Xers to look for companies that had mentoring programs. Still, Gen X would not have turned down mentorship from a more experienced colleague they trusted and respected.

Millennials are distinct in their assertiveness in asking for support. They can make great mentees. They work well with others. They are highly collaborative and open about their hopes and dreams. Having had parents and teachers that always engaged them in open dialogue, millennials have no issue with building rapport with authority figures. On the contrary, they will engage authority figures directly and have no hesitation about speaking their mind. And that right there is what sets them apart—their willingness to ask for things and make their demands known.

Companies are listening. Unfortunately, for the millennials, this is a case of "be careful what you wish for." Millennials asked for mentors. What they got were formal *mentorship programs*. When the assigned pairings lead to a relationship based on connection and trust, they can offer memorable and rewarding experiences. When they don't, both parties can walk away disillusioned or frustrated.

Clearly, we prefer the former. The question, then, is—how can organizations do better?

Issue Advice—Foster Mentorship

Mentoring relationships are the most intimate professional relationships most people will ever experience. Taking someone under your wing is no small thing. It takes time and work, given freely and enthusiastically. Most people will readily mentor someone they believe in. I would like us all to get to a point in life and have experiences as both mentors and mentees; I just don't think it prudent to start a relationship with that being the expectation. Instead, we should arrive at that conclusion, over time, together.

The core issue with formalized mentorship programs is they can put the cart before the horse, presuming the pairing will lead to connection and trust. These programs may not address issues of compatibility or relevance, and they fail to address the expectations each party is bringing to the new relationship. Being in an assigned relationship where the power dynamic is inherently asymmetric can also be a cause for concern. This is one of the reasons calling people that participate in these programs *mentors* may be counterproductive. The term *mentor* implies an intimacy that hasn't been established. Companies often fail to clearly establish how it defines mentoring. The concept is usually defined by the administrators of the program when it is "launched," but in practice, everyone comes to the party with their own interpretation of what it means to them.

I previously addressed the distinction between mentoring and sponsoring, mentoring being a more supportive, advice-based exchange and sponsoring being more proactive and advocacy-based. While these distinctions may be clear to a person like myself who has spent time learning about each process, others not familiar with the definitions might mistakenly expect some degree of sponsorship from a mentor. This is a subject for ongoing discussion as the relationship develops; advocacy requires trust and trust is built over time.

Companies would be better served using language not so steeped in unrealistic expectations. If someone offered to set you up on a blind date you might say yes (depending on your faith in your friend's judgment, prior track record, etc.). But if that same friend offered to select and assign your future spouse—sight unseen—you would likely decline (and probably ask if your friend had been drinking). The latter implies a serious obligation and a tremendous leap of faith, the former a relatively low-risk experiment. It's why the best advice for a blind date is to meet for coffee (vs. dinner), to minimize the initial commitment.

Companies should consider the impact of the term *mentor* as it is dripping with expectations and implied commitment. Instead of *mentorship programs,* consider calling them *advisory programs* or *guidance programs* or whatever culturally normed language your firm embraces. Calling these programs *advisory programs* is far less assuming and much more accurate. It sets a lower bar in terms of expectations that reduces the possibility of disappointment by either party. And some—hopefully many—of these advisors will evolve over time to become mentors.

When someone is new to an organization, an advisor issuing practical advice is exactly what that worker needs. A mentor can provide support and deep insight that propels the mentee forward in their career. This is incredibly valuable, but it's not what someone needs when they are learning the ropes. People new to their role are on a learning curve. They need support when something is working and detailed feedback when it is not. The benefit of someone helping to chart a career path and shepherd them to the next role can and should come later.

Advisor programs should be structured to suit the needs of their participants. Anyone entering a new position can benefit from supportive onboarding programs that ease these transitions. Staff these programs with advisors available for consultation, intimacy not required. Some companies already do this by providing new employees with a "buddy." The buddy system matches a new employee with someone who has been working at the firm for a year or two. Having someone available who can recall their first few months on the job gives the new employee access to a valuable resource. Workers new to their role need direction and feedback. They need someone to correct their mistakes and let them know when they are on the right track. Anyone new to a task responds well to this kind of feedback. Millennials, in particular, may appreciate the frequent check-ins. Gen Xers may be less interested in regular interaction, instead preferring less frequent contact with an advisor. Not everyone conforms to generational trends. Embrace people's differences by allowing them to adjust the frequency and mode of interaction to suit their needs.

While these advisor programs may not directly result in mentoring relationships, they do create an environment in which those relationships can bloom. They can also serve as a bridge; the advisor, once he or she has come to know the employee, would have an informed point of view regarding which of the more tenured members of the organization might be an appropriate mentor. The likelihood of success based on the advisor's recommendation would certainly be higher than the results for a near-random pairing. Let me be clear, I have no truck with mentoring, but I firmly believe in a stepped approach. Advisors, buddies, or as Dr. Carol Sanford, author of *The Regenerative Business* would call *resources*, are all people within the firm who are willing to pay it forward by sharing their knowledge and experience with others. Asking for and receiving help on a regular basis is the foundation of the mentoring relationships. These relationships help people succeed and move forward in their careers; mentors provide personal advice and targeted insights that no one else can. These relationships have to be nurtured over time.

Successful organizations with strong leadership already have plenty of potential mentors in their ranks. Good managers tend to make good mentors. Hire managers that care for their team members. Promote people into management that take an interest in people. Not only will they be better team leaders, but they are also often the type of people that will want to serve as a mentor for the right person. Build in unstructured time at work so that the mentors can easily mentor others without overtaxing themselves. Make it a line item in that time is allotted to, as Nucor would describe it, "building people." Support mentors and would-be mentors however you can. Consider establishing relationship-building programs that focus on developing the conversational skills essential to building mentoring relationships. Make mentoring a core value of the firm by instituting a recognition program for people at the firm who have contributed to the growth and development of fellow employees. John Campbell, the author of *The Power of Myths* said, "If you really want to help this world, what you will have to teach is how to live in it." Create narratives about mentoring experiences that—through examples—express its criticality to helping people succeed. Weave these principles into the organization's culture.

Some people make better advisors and others make better mentors. Boomers are often eager to serve as mentors to the young, but they don't always make good skill builders. They speak from a place of mastery. It may have been decades since they did the kind of work that young millennials are doing. The very nature of work has changed so much that boomers might have never had to do the work that their young reports do on a daily basis. They are likely to remember the *feeling* of doing the work, but not necessarily the details, and so they speak to the former more than the latter. While it can be helpful to be mentored on the nature of work as one advances through one's career, people new to their roles need to learn how to do the job.

Boomers tend to give big-picture guidance rather than

practical advice. Rather than advising you on how to do the work, they will instead talk to you about the "nature" of the work. This kind of big-picture advice can seem detached or removed from the actual work young people do on the job. For these reasons, boomers need to be cognizant of the actual needs of their young millennials. I believe we boomers are better suited to be mentors for Gen Xers and millennials who are further along in their careers.

On average, second-wave Gen Xers and first wave millennials will be better suited than boomers to serve as advisors and perhaps even mentors for younger millennials. Gen Xers are now often the managers for millennials in the nation's workforce. Gen Xers *are* willing to be mentors. Some of them might just be averse to "too much too soon" if the other party has different assumptions as to the depth of the mentoring relationship. Gen X will likely be more welcoming of advisory programs as they don't imply the same level of commitment and expectation. They may find themselves more willing to become actual mentors over time. First-wave millennials are serving as advisors and have been doing so for quite some time. Fortunately for them, Gen Zers also seem amenable to advisory programs that don't require a deep relational commitment, but this point is speculative as they are just entering the workplace in large numbers. Luckily for Gen Z, millennials tend to give support and mentorship because they wanted it so bad themselves. How receptive Gen Zers will be to advice remains an open question.

The intergenerational nature of mentoring cannot be overstated. Mentorship involves the passing of the baton from one generation to the next. This is not so different from a relay race where runners pass the baton from one to the next. The handoff is steady and sequential; they don't skip runners. Companies will have more success in supporting and nurturing young workers by recognizing and leveraging the diverse generational cohorts in the workplace.

Whatever approach your company chooses to employ in the pursuit of knowledge transfer and one-on-one development, remember that words matter. Mentoring is a big word with big expectations attached. Many mentoring success stories are fully appreciated only in hindsight. Think carefully about how to create the conditions for personal connections to be made across experience levels and generational cohorts. A layered, advisor/mentor approach deserves consideration. Remind your experienced team members that the person sitting across from them sees and experiences the world differently than they do. Encourage them to make time to listen and get to know their colleagues. Embrace and accept their expectations and motivations. They are with you because you have the ability to help them navigate the workplace and chart a course, with your help, to winning their working life version of *The $10,000 Pyramid*.

Conclusions

Conclusions

"The only reality I can possibly know is the world as I perceive it at this moment. The only reality you can possibly know is the world as you see it at this moment. And the only certainty is that those perceived realities are different. There are as many 'real worlds' as there are people!"

Carl Rogers

Dear reader, first, I want to thank you for taking the time to read what I had to say about generational dynamics at work. I hope you found it time well spent.

I have always considered the discussion of generational dynamics to be only one aspect of embracing diversity and furthering inclusion in the workplace. This is a gateway issue and possibly a template for recognizing and overcoming the differences in other parts of our lives. Knowing that we have more in common than that which separates us makes talking about generational differences relatively easy. You have your experiences growing up, I have mine; I share mine and you share yours. It can and should be a very meaningful, ongoing conversation, because as a consequence you know me a little better and I, in turn, learn more about you. We might even examine our original assumptions and better understand why we held them, why they might be misinformed, and what we need to do going forward. Hopefully, we become a bit more forgiving, or at the very least, a bit more patient when frustrations arise.

I am not so naïve to think one book on one aspect of our possible differences fundamentally changes how we interact. Returning to the water analogies, the author James N. Watkins expressed it nicely when he said, "A river cuts through rock not because of its power but because of its persistence. If a rock represents an obstacle to overcoming differences then we, all of us, must persist in our efforts to know and understand each other. If you are a manager, leader, or a person in a position of power, start a conversation with your colleagues and share the story of how you grew up and what was expected of you. And now, based on what has worked for you, what you expect of others and what do they expect of you in return. Why start with the leader or manager? Hopefully, the manager or leader creates the circumstances for "implicit reciprocity." This means that if I tell you a bit about myself and I shape the narrative in a way that emphasizes my personal history and how that history has informed how I work with people, then you, the listener, may very well share yours. This approach is especially important when the power dynamics in the relationship are asymmetrical. The leader, by telling their story, is giving permission for others to tell theirs and at the same time is shaping, by inference of their own narrative, what they would like to learn.

The operative word is conversation. Conversations are how we connect more deeply with those who work with us. Engaging dialogues with coworkers about the possibly of having different generational views is a gateway issue and a template for discussing other possible differences between us. It is also relevant to something we rarely talk about at work—*love*. Interestingly, we can say something grand such as "love your fellow man (and woman)," or "I love this job," but what we don't do is profess love to individual colleagues, and I am certainly not suggesting that you do.

What I am suggesting is love isn't an expression at work, it is an action. It reminds me of an improvisational theater game called the "hidden want," where two people are on a stage about to begin a scene. Rather than script the scene, each person has a "hidden want." It might be that one person's hidden want is to be seen as important, and the other person might have a want to be seen as kind. During the scene, she would never say she is important, nor would he say he is kind, it is their behaviors that align with their wants, not the statement of the want, thus it is hidden. He now feels she must be important by the way she acts and he in turn is felt by her to be kind.

Before your next conversation entertain the notion of having the "hidden want" of being understanding. When someone feels understood, they feel validated and hopefully more open to you and your views. In its own small way, this is an act of love. Being listened to and listening in return brings us closer together. I begin to understand the person before me. I needn't rely on the generalizations or heuristics I use on any given day when I go about categorizing fellow employees I don't yet know. We see individuals for who they truly are, and they feel seen in return. The popular vernacular would describe it as "she gets me."

I was never much for grand gestures. For me, it is the little kindnesses that accumulate over time that are true demonstrations of caring. I have no argument with holiday parties, or bonuses, or company outings, but give me a manager who sees me for who I truly am and helps me become who I am capable of being, then I could live without many of the other trappings of office life. This is Organizational Behavior 101. The trappings are satisfiers, in that you are either satisfied or not satisfied if there was a holiday party or if your raise was a 5, 7, or 9 percent increase. These are extrinsic rewards, and they have their place since we are, by nature, comparative in our situations relative to others.

Extrinsic rewards become especially important in a transactional world where employees compare what is offered against what employees feel they deserve, but they are not by themselves motivating; they become expectations that *satisfy*. Motivators on the other hand are intrinsic; they come from within. If you, as a manager, in the day-to-day, show that you care about who I am, that you care about how I am doing, and are willing to help me do it better, then that, dear reader is motivating. It makes the work itself enjoyable and rewarding, knowing that as the employee gains mastery she is recognized for the contributions she is making.

These actions taken by a manager on behalf of an employee are not just motivating, they contribute to creating what is called "psychological safety." Amy Edmondson, a professor of leadership and management at the Harvard Business School, defines it as "a workplace where one feels that one's voice is welcome with bad news, questions, concerns, half-baked ideas, and even mistakes."[21] There are two criteria that need to be present in order to

---

21 Corey Stieg, "Psychological safety at work improves productivity—here are 4 ways to get it, according to a Harvard expert," *CNBC*, October 4, 2020, https://www.cnbc.com/2020/10/05/why-psychological-safety-is-important-at-work-and-how-to-create it.html#:~:text=Psychological%20safety%20describes%20%22a%20workplace,pitch%20ideas%20without%20undue%20repercussions.

create this space: a feeling of belonging and of having the ability and confidence to contribute. Ability, as previously discussed, is your role as a teacher providing them with feedback that recognizes and develops their unique strengths and contributions that I characterized as embracing their "lopsidedness." Belonging is a layered term in that the individual feels at one level they belong, as in a valued member of the department or team, and furthermore, that they belong to something larger, something that gives purpose to the work they do.

I probably could have discussed all of this without using the word *love*. Empathy, caring, respect, kindness, or simple consideration for others would have sufficed. So why did I? After all, this is a business book, not a dating manual. It certainly wasn't for shock value or that I am exceptionally sentimental. I bring it up, dear reader, because the young have gotten used to hearing it. It seems that outside of work, the use of the word *love* has proliferated at home.

As I established at the beginning of this book and throughout, I am a boomer. I have been speaking on this topic with a modicum of expertise for roughly two decades, and I often ask select audiences several questions when I speak. My first query is, "Has anyone in the audience sired children or have children in their lives they love?" If I get lots of audience members saying yes, I continue with the next question. I ask, "Do you tell them you love them?" This is usually met with a blustery chorus of, "of course we do," as if I had asked a ridiculous follow-up question. Lastly, I ask, "How often do you tell them that you love them?" The replies range from "daily" to "every time we speak."

I then switch gears and ask the boomers in the room, "How often did your parents say, 'I love you'?" Crickets. Generally, I am met with silence, or I receive the occasional responses: "on holidays" or after "funerals." Were we loved? Yes, of course, we were. It was inferred, but not commonly expressed. Yet we have now raised both millennials and Gen Zers with daily doses of "I love you." We have now made the implicit explicit. Frankly, hearing you are loved trumps guessing you are. And this is only a small part of the "concerted cultivation" they were likely to have experienced growing up. It is why in lieu of telling your young employees they are loved, which I would never recommend, I would recommend taking actions that align with a reasonable workplace approximation of showing you care. This discussion brings us back to the gateway issue and the template.

This book was not only meant to shine a light on that which makes each generation unique, but it also contains a number of suggestions on how to bridge our differences. As I said, this topic is a gateway issue. There are other issues the workplace grapples with that include racial, gender, sexuality, ethnic, socioeconomic, and religious differences. All of these issues need to be addressed not only because it is the right thing to do but because organizations, businesses, and the nation are better as a consequence of embracing our differences. We are creating the habit of intentional inquiry for purposes of understanding, surfacing, and eliminating any false assumptions we hold of others. This becomes our template for resolving differences. Much like Organizational Behavior 101, it is Negotiations 101 in how to navigate our relationship in a way that is win-win for all involved.

When entering into a negotiation always start where it's easy for both parties to reach an agreement. Considering the challenges faced with making the workplace more inclusive and more diverse, talking about how you were raised and how it shaped who you are and how you work will go a long way toward setting the stage for other conversations about our differences. This type of conversation is relatively easy once you get the hang of it, and we are likely to discover we aren't so different after all.

And finally, I close with one more piece of advice about dealing with (and avoiding) assumptions. When in doubt about some irritating action or behavior you have observed in another, imagine for a moment he or she is a rational person (like yourself) and the action taken, as seen by them, was rational. You needn't agree with the action, but you do need to give them *the benefit of the doubt* and make an effort to understand why they took it. So, the next time when you are tilting your head and trying to figure out why—just ask. You may discover what you initially saw as a problem was simply a different way of looking at things, a new and possibly fresh perspective that is a direct outcome of embracing generational diversity.

Acknowledgments

Acknowledgments

When I first started to speak on the topic of intergenerational friction at work nearly two decades ago, I was occasionally asked if I had written a book. My initial reaction was one of surprise, as in "Me, write a book?" Over time I thought more and more about the possibility of doing so, but I, like most people, am lopsided. Though I am comfortable presenting or training, I was not entirely confident I could write a book. When I finally committed to doing so, I realized I would need help. It is those people who brought my aspiration to fruition whom I would like to thank.

First off, I'd like to thank Hobbs Allison, Julia Steffy, Brandon Coward, Nicole Hall, Shannon Sullivan, Jennifer Schwartz, and—last but not least—Naren Aryal, CEO of Amplify Publishing, for their valuable input and for shepherding me through the process. A special thanks to Kristin Taylor, my exceptional developmental editor, who insisted I speak from the heart.

I also received valuable advice in how to express and shape my message from close friends. Let me start with my brother, Mark De Santis, for writing the foreword. When I broached the subject of writing a book, he had faith in me before I had faith in myself. Next is the ever-generous Benvenuti family—Leo, Joy, their daughter Leigh, and their son Jack for injecting joy (no pun intended) into the manuscript. I'd also like to thank my longtime friend Gus Buktenica, an actor, writer, and all-around good guy who helped me stay true to my voice. Lastly, my dearest friend, Jorge Cauz, who not only provided me with invaluable feedback from the prospective of keeping the topic relevant to business professionals but encouraged me when I was making progress and prodded me along when I was not.

As I said, I am by my own definition lopsided, and so I reached out to two amazingly talented individuals for help in putting words to paper. Andrew Mortazavi, a writer by training and experience, took my concepts, my notes, and spoken words and made them into a cogent, thoughtful, and uniquely expressed manuscript. Tim McClure—a strategist and occasional business partner—took the manuscript, added his own insights, and enlivened it in ways I had never considered. I am very grateful for their significant contributions, which is why Andrew and Tim are also named on the cover of this book.

Chris De Santis

March 2021

chris@cpdesantis.com